"*A Pastor's Toolbox 2* is an invaluable resource and a welcome addition to any parish library!"

> —Most Rev. Bernard Hebda
> Archbishop of Minneapolis-St. Paul

"Once again the National Leadership Roundtable has produced a resource guide for those involved in church/parish management. Like the first volume, this work continues to build upon the foundation of that workshop. Offering guidance and direction that benefits a priest administrator daily in his ministry, it is a book that should be gifted to every new pastor—if not every newly ordained priest."

> —Rev. John M. McCrone
> Director, Continuing Formation and Sabbaticals
> Archdiocese of Newark

"The first volume of *A Pastor's Toolbox* was received with gratitude and enthusiasm by priests and bishops across the country. This second can, indeed, help any new pastor as he approaches the management of his parish. As a companion to the first, new and seasoned pastors have the answers to so many questions regarding parochial leadership. I have seen firsthand the positive difference the first edition has made and can heartily recommend both volumes!"

> —Cardinal Joseph Tobin, C.Ss.R.
> Archbishop of Newark

A Pastor's Toolbox 2

*More Management Skills
for Parish Leadership*

Edited by Paul A. Holmes

LITURGICAL PRESS
Collegeville, Minnesota

www.litpress.org

1	2	3	4	5	6	7	8	9

Library of Congress Cataloging-in-Publication Data

Names: Holmes, Paul A., editor.
Title: A pastor's toolbox 2 : more management skills for parish leadership / edited by Paul A. Holmes.
Other titles: Pastor's toolbox two
Description: Collegeville, Minnesota : Liturgical Press, 2017.
Identifiers: LCCN 2017004823 (print) | LCCN 2017023029 (ebook) | ISBN 9780814645055 (ebook) | ISBN 9780814646700
Subjects: LCSH: Pastoral theology—Catholic Church. | Christian leadership—Catholic Church. | Parishes.
Classification: LCC BX1913 (ebook) | LCC BX1913 .P3482 2017 (print) | DDC 254—dc23
LC record available at https://lccn.loc.gov/2017004823

Contents

Foreword

Archbishop Bernard Hebda
Archdiocese of St. Paul and Minneapolis

It is no secret that Catholic pastors everywhere enjoy one of the most rewarding ministries in the church. It is equally well known that they face many challenges whether they are shepherding a large urban parish or a small rural one; whether they minister with a paid, professional management team or a staff of lay volunteers; whether stewardship efforts have created a deep pool of resources that can fund a complex set of programs and ministerial experiences, or the parish is struggling mightily to meet its financial obligations. Leading and managing a Catholic parish in the twenty-first century asks a great deal from its pastor. That is why *A Pastor's Toolbox 2* is an invaluable resource and a welcome addition to any parish library!

I had the pleasure of attending a weeklong Toolbox for Pastoral Management experience in January 2016, led by Fr. Paul Holmes, the insightful editor of this volume. Thirty pastors from the Archdiocese of Newark spent six days together getting acquainted with one another, yes, but also with the management tools needed to meet many of the challenges pastors face. A few months later, I invited the Leadership Roundtable to bring the Toolbox to the Archdiocese of St. Paul and Minneapolis as well. Those two privileged opportunities have given me firsthand knowledge of just how helpful the Toolbox can be for both new and seasoned pastors, and I know that my experience was not unique. I remember seeing a photo that accompanied a *New York Times* article about the Toolbox: the priest-participants were obviously enjoying the experience of listening to leadership and management specialists share their expertise. Volume 2 of *A Pastor's Toolbox* provides a glimpse into that experience.

There are many books out there that address organizational leadership and management. Very few, however, speak directly to the Catholic pastor, and in a language that respects his theological, spiritual, and pastoral training. It is one thing to advise a leader to be consultative; it is quite another to root that advice in the notion that we Christians are the Body of Christ: "If we look at Jesus' methodology of calling apostles to share in leadership, it becomes clear that a collaborative style of leadership is pivotal to Christian management" (chap. 4: Molding Your Staff into a Pastoral Leadership Team).

While all effective leaders may seek wisdom, the Catholic pastor does so for a reason that would not occur to a secular leader: "Council members want to be consulted so they can express and unfold the wisdom of Christ. Ultimately, the Holy Spirit unifies pastor and council members when they develop plans that the pastor wants to implement" (chap. 6: The Pastoral Council and Consultative Leadership).

Indeed, while many nonprofit leaders are engaged in raising money, the pastor needs to remember that "living a stewardship life is a manifestation of mature discipleship. It is a conscious decision to follow Christ no matter what the cost" (chap. 8: Ten Essential Building Blocks for Developing a Stewardship Parish). It is not enough, we are reminded, to ensure that parish communications be well written; pastors have to give it their very best: "Our desire for communion should compel us to be not just good communicators, but *Gospel-good* communicators" (chap. 9: Communications: Vitamins or Dessert?).

Only a book that speaks directly to Catholic pastors (and not just *any* leader) would make the following observation: "We need to develop reflective leaders. Priests are particularly good at this. It's part of the formation that we go through as Catholic ministry leaders—where solutions emerge from prayer, discernment, and dialogue. Solutions emerge over time with reflection" (chap. 10: Tools for Leadership Development). And the pastor should not be the only one praying: "Finance council members are also expected to invest in developing a robust prayer life that includes asking guidance of the Holy Spirit, and participation in the liturgical life of the parish" (chap. 5: Frameworks and Tools That Drive the Parish Finance Council). The entire parish, in fact, should be basing their decisions on what they have learned in prayer: "Intentionally inviting the Holy Spirit into our minds and hearts changes us and has the power to change our conversations. We are able to do more and do it based on the will of God (instead of our own will) when we spend time listening to what God has to say to us first instead of us speaking first or, perhaps even worse, not listening at all" (chap. 7: Effective Parish Meetings).

It is evident that the wisdom of our Holy Fathers is an integral part of the book as well. Catholic pastors cannot help but benefit from the insights of Pope Francis (chaps. 1, 2, 7, 9, 10, 12, 14, 15) as well as those of his immediate predecessors, St. John Paul (chaps. 5, 6, 14) and Pope Benedict (chaps. 8, 9, 14).

I hope it is clear, even from this brief outline, that *A Pastor's Toolbox* does not forget its audience. It doesn't simply provide those who lead parishes, whether ordained or lay, with management tools that would work just *anywhere*. Instead, we are uniquely addressed as true *ecclesial* ministers. Grounded in our baptismal identity and mission, we lead and manage our parishes in service to Christ's identity and mission. I can, therefore, wholeheartedly recommend this volume's sixteen essays to all who hope to equip themselves with the tools that Catholic parish management needs to ensure the vibrant parish life our parishioners deserve.

Introduction

Paul A. Holmes

Welcome to the second volume of *A Pastor's Toolbox*!

None of us involved with the Toolbox for Pastoral Management could have imagined the success of the first volume of *A Pastor's Toolbox: Management Skills for Parish Leadership*, published by Liturgical Press in 2014. And we couldn't have been more grateful when the Catholic Press Association awarded it First Prize in its Pastoral Ministry category. A collaborative effort of Seton Hall University and the Leadership Roundtable (formerly, the National Leadership Roundtable on Church Management), the weeklong, face-to-face Toolbox for Pastoral Management continues to be offered all around the country and will have soon reached five hundred priests and deacons ministering in over seventy-five dioceses in the United States and Canada.

Since 2009, a member of the Leadership Roundtable's board of directors, Thomas Healey, has been both the inspiration for the Toolbox and its most generous supporter. It was he who encouraged us to publish the seminar's presentations in book form. In this way, he said, we would be able to reach the more than thirty-five thousand active priests in the US, as well as the nearly forty thousand lay ecclesial ministers who might benefit from the Toolbox's presentations on the many facets of parish temporal management.[1] And over the years, we have been grateful to Lilly Endowment's generosity in support of the mission and goals of the Toolbox experience.

New pastors, especially, have told us that they received enough "theory" in the seminary; now, they say, they want practical "tools" that will help them hit the ground running as they set about managing their parishes—tools that are grounded in sound Catholic theology and that truly help pastors bring Christ to the faithful in their care. In the first volume of *A Pastor's Toolbox*, we offered tools of temporal management, including subjects as diverse as how to manage the parish business office, how to handle the hiring and nurturing of parish staff, and what to do about risk management, internal financial controls, stewardship, and strategic planning, among others. We've continued to listen to the feedback we've received from those who have attended the Toolbox seminars and, here in the second volume, we offer essays replete with tools that pastors say they would like to have in their "toolbox" as they go about their management responsibilities in a twenty-first-century Catholic parish.

We begin with Dominic Perri, who tries to answer the question a lot of pastors are asked: What is your vision for our parish? He tells pastors that "mission" is about identity, but "vision" is about where you want to go in the future (chap. 1). Barbara Anne Cusack then helps us to understand that undergirding the pastor's vision should be an appreciation for what the church's own law might be able to tell us, especially if we seek inspiration from the Holy Spirit and view the law as a bridge instead of a burden (chap. 2).

Pastors have told us how much effort goes into the management of a parish's human resources, so Carol Fowler helps pastors to "get a handle" on some of the pastor's most important and time-consuming tasks, giving advice on hiring (and firing), benefits and compensation, avoiding the various forms of discrimination, and the benefits of having a personnel handbook (chap. 3). Dovetailing with those insights are Dennis Corcoran's view of "molding" the parish staff into a real leadership team whose members need to be relational, open to change, and working to achieve the "right chemistry" with their pastor, with one another, and with their fellow parishioners (chap. 4).

We then zero in on the tools needed to manage the important work a pastor does in consultation with his parishioners on the parish's finance and pastoral councils. Jim Lundholm-Eades offers an incisive perspective: "'Best practice' finance councils use consistent frames of reference to guide what they do, and a pragmatic set of tools to get the work done" (chap. 5). Mark Fischer and Fr. Paul Spellman then offer best practices when it comes to the pastoral council, inviting us to view the council as the "'eyes and ears' of the parish" and emphasizing how pastors need to be "consultative leaders" (chap. 6). And since consultation most often occurs at meetings, Peter Denio presents tools for making all parish meetings as effective as possible, adapting the perspective of business management consultant Patrick Lencioni to parish life (chap. 7).

In addition to meetings, pastors find themselves involved in strategies for managing parish stewardship. Chuck Zech, of Villanova's Center for Church Management and Business Ethics, offers ten essential building blocks for developing a "stewardship parish" (chap. 8). Helen Osman then suggests that "parishes (and dioceses) should think of communications as essential an element to the church's ministry as vitamins are to a healthy person's daily diet." How we communicate "who we are" and "what we do" as members of Christ's Body is critical as the church tries to offer a "clear vision" of our ecclesial identity and mission to the communities we serve (chap. 9).

All pastors can benefit from considering how they are developing as leaders, managing their time, and attending to both their emotional and physical well-being. Michael Brough provides tools for leadership development, focusing on identifying a pastor's leadership competencies, gathering feedback, creating a development plan, and engaging the support that is needed to be a truly effective leader (chap. 10). Jim Dubik offers insights about how to manage one's time, reminding us that management is about efficiency and that all leaders need to develop a "time management system" and do their best to stick to it (chap. 11). And as pastors go about their management tasks, they mustn't forget about their health. Dr. Andrew Kelly discusses the many ways our physical and emotional lives might get lost in the flurry of pastoral activity. He offers a "wellness checklist" that reminds pastors to take care of themselves so that they can take care of others (chap. 12).

Many parishes find themselves in special circumstances. Those that have a Catholic school, for example, often need to consider various strategies that will help ensure that the religious education of our children has the pastor's care-filled attention. John Eriksen offers strategies like advocacy, building a skilled support network, and benchmarking to help ensure the success of the parish school (chap. 13). Increasingly, faith communities require what might be called "complex pastoring" due to the increase of multiple parishes and cultural communities in an individual pastor's care. Mark Mogilka offers strategies for building bridges among parish communities, reminding us that "change that you can see and touch—is easy; but transition—changing people's hearts, attitudes, beliefs, and values—takes a lot more time and patience" (chap. 14). Father Allan Deck notes that pastors are, more and more, in need of "intercultural competence" and he reminds us that in order to model intercultural sensibility and competence, we may need not only a change of "mind-set" but a change of "heart-sets" and "skill-sets" as well (chap. 15).

Finally, Dennis Cheesebrow offers a word about managing change, on both individual and institutional levels (chap. 16). In every pastor's toolbox there should be the tools that can effect the kinds of transformation to which every parish is called. As we said in the first volume of *A Pastor's Toolbox*, we say now: There are many more issues facing twenty-first-century pastors and parishioners. It is nevertheless our hope that the issues we have tackled in both volumes might be considered a road map to grace-filled moments, filled with Christ's love and wisdom, for everyone involved in parish life.

Endnote

1. CARA (Center for Applied Research in the Apostolate), Georgetown University, "Frequently Requested Church Statistics," http://cara.georgetown.edu/frequently-requested-church-statistics/.

1

Developing a Vision

Dominic Perri

Proverbs 29 tells us, "Where there is no vision, the people perish" (v. 18, King James Version). I wouldn't say that most parishes today are on the verge of extinction. What I would suggest, though, is that they are hungry for vision. What exactly do I mean by vision, and how is it different from mission? If you've asked that question yourself and are lost for an answer, you're not alone. I hear it all the time.

Very simply, your mission is a statement of identity. It's who you are as a parish, or any other type of ministry. We are, for example, the Parish of St. Mary's. And we exist to preach and teach the sacraments and bring the Gospel to those in our community. As a statement of identity, it generally does not change, nor should it change, at least for decades. To relate this to the for-profit world, take a company like Nike. It's always going to be a shoe seller and a provider of athletic goods. That's not going to change from one year to the next. It's a fundamental statement of corporate identity.

Vision, on the other hand, is where you want to go in the future. It's the ability to say, "We're at point A and want to get to point B." It's where you're trying to lead people. Vision is what I call a *desired future*. To personalize that a bit, I'm the son of Italian immigrants who grew up in Louisville, Kentucky, of all places. That's my identity. I can't change that. But my vision of where I wanted to go has changed over my life. I was determined to go to college, so I enrolled in The Catholic University of America. After graduation, I wanted to leave my mark in the workplace, then get married and start a family. My vision involved setting goals for myself, moving toward them, and setting new goals. Unlike mission, your vision changes over time.

How many of you have had people come up and ask, "What's your vision for the parish?" As pastors, your vision is to lead your people. But where do you want to take them? That's where your vision is crucial. The faithful are basically asking, "Where do you see yourself taking us?" It seems very simple. We start at point A and go to point B. That's what vision is. That's what leading is.

But it's not as simple as it appears. Anyone who's ever been part of drafting a vision statement for an organization knows what I'm talking about. Too often, what ultimately gets produced is tacked on the wall like the Declaration of Independence; it looks very pretty, but that's essentially the end of the story. The process is often difficult and wrenching and the toughest part is afterward when people say, "I don't know what we got out of this. I don't know how it changed our organization." So, what I want to really focus on is helping you think about and create a vision that will allow you to move your parish to where you want it to be. And hopefully without the pain and aggravation I'm sure many of you have experienced.

Knowing What Road to Take

Why is vision so important? There's no better instructor here than Lewis Carroll, who, in *Alice in Wonderland*, describes a scene where Alice encounters the Cheshire Cat. As many of you will recall, Alice asks for directions: "Would you tell me, please, which way I ought to go from here?" The Cheshire Cat replies, "That depends a good deal on where you want to get to." When Alice says she doesn't really know where she wants to go, the Cat famously replies, "Then it doesn't matter which way you go."[1]

The message is clear: If you don't know where you want to go, then you drift. And as I've seen through my experiences with parishes around the country, there are many in various stages of drift. They're in maintenance mode. It's akin to treading water. And this, unfortunately, leads to a bit of a leadership and vision vacuum. So that when well-intentioned folks in the parish show up with a bright and shiny idea, the feeling is maybe we should pursue it. Since we don't know where we're going, any road will get us there. It's the polar opposite of having a vision that allows you to say, "This is where we're going . . . or not going." With respect to the latter, it might be a great program. It may have worked well in another parish. You may be very excited about it. But with vision as your guide, you may also realize that it's not appropriate for your parish. Just as importantly, though, it allows you to refocus, to move decisively in a new direction.

To give you another perspective, George Wilson, a friend and mentor of mine, is a Jesuit who did organization development work with church groups for over thirty years. He has stated that many church organizations don't have a resource problem; they have a *vison* problem. It's no secret that many Catholic parishes and organizations spend a lot of time lamenting how strapped they are for funds, and how hard it is to attract competent people to their ranks. But that's hardly the end of the discussion. I believe we have to ask ourselves a very fundamental question: Are we putting out a product with a compelling enough vision to attract people and resources to us? In the end, people want to be part of something that's going somewhere, and if it appears we're just treading water, that we're in perpetual maintenance mode, then they're going to turn away from the church in droves.

What, then, should our vision be? How do we get people enthused about our "product"? Our lofty vision for our parish is typically to bring all souls to Jesus. The problem is that it doesn't necessarily give you a direction for where you want to be tomorrow or next month or next year. In other words, it doesn't give you a vision—a desired future—that can help you plan and make decisions for your parish.

Here's an example from the secular world that may help. Consider film directors. They must have a very clear sense of what the final product is going to look like, even if it hasn't been created yet. They have a *desired future*. This is the kind of product we want. Think of yourselves as directors creating a film. You may be shooting seven scenes in three cities—let's say Los Angeles, Chicago, and Newark. But if scenes one and five are in Los Angeles, you don't go to Los Angeles for scene one, then the other cities for scenes two, three, and four, only to return to Los Angeles for scene five. That wouldn't make any sense. You shoot scenes one and five in Los Angeles in tandem. The point is, directors must have in mind what the final product is going to look like in order to pull off that kind of logistical exercise. Since it's not happening in sequence, they need to see the bigger picture through the smaller component parts in each city. Indeed, if you listen to interviews with directors, they will invariably say, "I knew what each scene had to deliver because I had the bigger picture of how they would all fit together in the end."

The question I pose to you as pastors and leaders in your parishes is this: Do you have a vision of what you want your parish to look like in three years? Can you look at the smaller parts of that mosaic right now and say, "They have to be this way because here is what the final product will look like"? That's the idea of vision. That's the idea of desired future.

Another example from the secular world is Apple. When the computer maker was founded, its vision was to get computers into the hands of everyday people, to make the devices accessible to every home. And the company succeeded beyond its wildest dreams. It had a vision of where it wanted to be. Its iconic leader, Steve Jobs, reinforced the point. After starting the company, he left, and returned when it almost went under in the mid-nineties. At that moment, Apple had roughly eighty-five products in its repertoire. Jobs drew a two-by-two matrix and said, "We're going to have four products—a desktop for home, a desktop for business, a laptop for home, and a laptop for business. We're getting rid of everything else." Not surprisingly, that sent a few shock waves through the organization. But that was the point at which Apple began to turn around and become the juggernaut it is today. Jobs had a very clear vision about where he wanted to take the company, and within a given time frame. He saw the future he wanted. And that's a powerful lesson for the church as well.

How a Vision Can Change

Let me give you an example that hits closer to home. My own parish—Old Saint Patrick's in downtown Chicago—dates back to the 1850s. By the early 1980s, it was on the verge of closing, a victim of the construction of the interstate highway system that tore neighborhoods apart and forced residents to flee. When Fr. Jack Wall took over as pastor in 1983, four members remained in the entire parish.

That would have sounded the death knell for most organizations, but Jack walked in and said, "I've got a vision for this parish. But it won't be like most parishes that are focused on attracting families and children. After all, we're in downtown Chicago, where nobody really lives. So we're going to become a place for young adults. Downtown Chicago is filled with young, single Catholic professionals who are coming to the city every day, and we can serve them in a host of ways—with programs at their lunch breaks and programs after work. We can tailor programs to them because they're now going to parishes in the suburbs, which are focused on families, and that's not who they are."

Jack had a bold vision, a desired future, for his parish. In some cases, that meant telling people, "We're not going to do this because it doesn't advance our vision." And in short order, amazing things began to happen. Young adults flocked there. One of the reasons was that Old Saint Pat's offered a Saturday night block party where people could go to eat, listen to bands, and mingle. I should note that these block parties raised money for the parish's social outreach program, so they were connected to the mission. Interestingly, what also happened at those block parties was that lots of young, single Catholic professionals started meeting each other, getting married, and having families.

And by 1989, when waves of Catholic parishes were closing their schools, Old Saint Pat's was just opening theirs. Today, it serves the needs of four thousand registered families from over sixty zip codes. And Jack will tell you that lots of people in those early years came to him and said, "How can you not have X, Y, Z—the standard way a parish serves families?" His answer was simple and direct: "That's not the future we're trying to get to."

There's no question your vision will change. It did for Apple and it did for Old Saint Pat's, once they started to grow and discovered they had different needs. Where it starts, though, is looking around and asking yourself, "Where are we now, and what will someone who shows up for Sunday Mass at our parish three years from now experience that's different?" Are you able to paint that picture? Can you talk about the desired future as the fulfillment of what you want your parish to become?

Vision brings that desired future into focus. And the other nice thing is that gifts and resources often follow in its wake. Just look at Old Saint Pat's. Each year its annual block party—now held on Friday *and* Saturday nights—attracts thousands of young people and raises several hundred thousand dollars each year. These contributions are then used to fund the church's social outreach programs. I'm not suggesting you come to the conclusion, "Oh my gosh, how do I ever come up with something like that!" What I am suggesting, though, is that when your vision, your desired future, is compelling enough, people and resources will inevitably follow.

Charting Your Course as a Parish

A clear vision also allows you to say *no* to certain things. And that's absolutely crucial. In your lives as pastors, how many times have people come up to you and said, "Father, I've got a great idea for our parish"? Or, "I just came back from this retreat and witnessed a program we have to have immediately." What's the measuring stick that allows you to say yes or no to each well-intentioned idea? Is it how much energy you have at the moment, or whether or not they caught you at the right time of the day? Absolutely not. Having a window into the future and being able to say to a member of your parish, "I appreciate your idea, but it doesn't quite line up with where we want this parish to be in another three years," should be your measuring stick.

Determining what you want your parish to become, of course, is no easy task. It means spending considerable time thinking about the needs of the people around you. What's unique about who we are as a parish? What's our history? How is the community changing? Setting a direction for the future means listening—to your staff, especially those who have been there the longest, to your parish council, to your parishioners, and to the community at large. You also need to study the demographic data. It may show, for example, you're in an area where Hispanics are the fastest growing population segment, prompting you to say, "We need to become a 100 percent bicultural English-Spanish parish. That's our desired future." What, then, will people experience when they come to our parish in another three years? Well, they'll see how we've managed to smoothly integrate the two cultures. There will be bilingual liturgies, bulletins in both English and Spanish, and active community outreach. And to get to that goal, we're going to start right now to build intercultural awareness through events, programs, and trips. That's how we plan to make our vision real.

Here's another example of what I mean by vision. In the course of listening and talking to others, you might come to see there's a hunger for a fuller expression of Catholic teachings on social justice. Therefore, your vision might be to convey that theme through parish preaching, or visits to local soup kitchens, or through faith-sharing groups where members reflect on how to embed Catholic social teachings in their everyday lives. That's the kind of experience you might want to build for parishioners, and your vision is the vehicle that will get you there.

There will always be folks who say, "No, no, Father. I don't think we should do it that way." And there's nothing preventing you from saying to them, "Here are my initial thoughts. Let's now take them to the parish council for its feedback." You can, and should, consult with others. At Old Saint Pat's, for example, we held a summit where we brought in seventy-five parish leaders for a day-and-a-half meeting to get input. At the end of the day, though, you are the leader of the parish and have to be able to say, "Based on what I've seen and heard, here is the direction in which we need to be moving. Here is where the Holy Spirit is beckoning us. Let's embark on this vision together."

One Church's Response

Church of the Nativity, a parish in the town of Timonium, Maryland, developed a very distinct vision of its desired future. Members looked around and realized they were in a sleepy northern suburb of Baltimore where the church really didn't matter in the lives of many people. So, they began by asking themselves some key questions: What experience do we want people to have when they come here on the weekend? How do we transform that personal experience from just sitting in a pew for forty-five minutes to actually becoming a disciple—to getting involved in a ministry, joining a small discussion group, or playing a role in community outreach? And, if we become a church filled with disciples, what activities need to occur throughout the week?

As members detailed in a book they eventually wrote about their journey called *Rebuilt*, they decided to concentrate on creating a dynamic, irresistible weekend experience. It featured programs for children and students, lots of music, and meaningful messages crafted by the church's ministers. In other words, they created the kind of engaging, energetic environment that would encourage newcomers to return and regular members to become even more active. To get to that level, though, they realized they'd have to really do their homework, planning the program and events for each Saturday and Sunday, weeks or even months in advance. They'd have to review the Scriptures and decide which lessons or themes to dwell on. And they'd have to thoughtfully integrate them with the weekend's music and hospitality.

In the course of saying yes to those ideas that would advance their vision, the parish also had the foresight—and strength—to say no to ideas that wouldn't. Bingo was one of those. So were CYO and sports. And to those people who objected to their choices, parish leaders politely suggested that Timonium might not be the right place for them, and guided them elsewhere.

Vision Takes Time and Patience

How do you know when you've arrived at a vision that can really energize your parish? Here's a simple yardstick: when you share your vision with people and they get excited about it. When they say, "Father, we want to be part of that," or "This is something we can buy into."

Be aware that developing the right vision for your parish may take some time. If you want a fully formed blueprint that fills your leaders with an unquenchable fire, one that really inspires people, it must be part of a deliberative, thoughtful, unhurried process. It must involve constant back-and-forth with those around you. In the course of that conversation you might learn, for example, there's a discernible desire to become a parish that lives and breathes the message of Pope Francis. Or to become a parish where young people feel especially welcome. Or a parish where *all* generations feel welcome. The core question then becomes, What do we need to do, or stop doing, to get us there?

Most important, don't be discouraged or sidetracked as you embark on this timely journey. As the leader of your congregation, continue to reflect on it and pray on it as you provoke a spirited discussion with the faithful. Stay focused and committed. Only then will a collective vision emerge with the energy to take your parish in a bold and exciting new direction, a desired future.

To paraphrase Proverbs 29, where there *is* a vision, the people flourish!

Endnote

1. Lewis Carroll, *Alice in Wonderland* (New York: Scholastic, 2001), 74.

The Pastor and Canon Law

Barbara Anne Cusack

The Code of Canon Law is fundamental to your role as pastor, helping to define your rights and obligations as well as an organizational structure without which it would be nearly impossible to govern. Like any body of law, canon law is also complex and because people approach it from so many different angles, it's useful to begin this discussion with some basic context. We have church law and we have canon law. Church law is bigger than canon law. It consists of conciliar legislation, postconciliar legislation, liturgical law, particular law for a diocese or a country, proper law if you're a member of a religious institute, and custom, which over a period of time can take on the weight of law. What we'll be focusing on in this chapter is the Code of Canon Law for the Catholic Church.

The Code is basically a codification of law within one volume. General law is the universal law of a church; it's binding regardless of where you are territorially. Particular law is for either a specific group or a specific location. We have particular law in the United States through the US Conference of Catholic Bishops, which establishes laws that are confirmed by the Vatican and are binding within the US. We also have personal law where religious, for example, have their own set of laws. And we have diocesan legislation.

Why do we even need law in the church if the church is about love? The answer is that the church and love are not in opposition. We have law to encourage, promote, and support life—the life of the individual and the life of the community, both now and in the future. Law is a servant of theology, just as theology is a servant of faith. If you think of theology as faith seeking understanding, think of law as theology seeking practice. Because law is subservient to theology, theology has to come first. You cannot read law outside of a theological context. If you do, you become very legalistic and don't understand the "whys" of what you're doing.

In areas where we have weak theology in the church, we may also have weak law. For example, Vatican II made an effort to begin talking differently about marriage, to talk about it in covenant language instead of contract language. The problem is, we haven't really succeeded in developing that theology. As a result, the law lags behind the theology. There's still a lot of contract language, which essentially works; it's not impeding anything. But not until the theology of marriage progresses and becomes more substantive in the life of the married couple—and that really means as covenant—will the law catch up.

The image I like to use for law, and the role of law in the church, is biblically based: the image of the church as the Body of Christ. Think about law—canon law—as the skeleton in the Body of Christ. It serves the same purposes as our own physical skeleton. It gives our body strength. It helps us move. We'd just be blobs on the floor if we didn't have our skeleton. It gives us support. And guess what? It's flexible.

The law has those same qualities. It exists to give support and structure to the church, to let individuals and bodies within the church move from one place to another. Think about it: if every time you sat down to deal with a case in the tribunal and had to think up a new procedure, you'd never get anywhere.

The Flexibility of Canon Law

How do we use law? Again, drawing on that image of the skeleton, the law is necessary but not sufficient for the life of the church. We may be divinely instituted, but we are also human, and if we didn't have some structure and some support we'd have a very hard time surviving as an institution. If all we had was the law, if the first thing people saw when they looked at the church was its law, then it would be as dead as the skeleton that hangs in a lab. It's not a living being.

The law itself is not sufficient for the church. It needs the flesh and blood and spirit to be the living church. As our physical bodies are flexible but become less so over time, so it is with the church's law. If I get a phone call from a pastor saying, "Here's my situation, what should I do?," I rarely say, "Do this." Instead, I say, "You can do everything from here to here and still be within the limits of the law." That's where the flesh and blood of the living church comes into play. You need to look at the situation through the prism of your experience and your knowledge of the people involved and decide where you are going to apply the law. Think again of your physical skeleton and the fact some bones are stronger than others. There's a reason your skull is the hardest bone in the body. It's because it protects something very important. If I break my finger it may be painful and inconvenient, but it's not life-threatening. But if I crack my skull, that's more serious. You need to look at law in the church in the same way. There are some laws that can't be bent, so you look at what's behind them. What value is the law protecting?

Let's consider the laws on sacraments. When the canons are dealing with matter and form of sacraments, they are quite firm. That's because they're protecting something very valuable to us, our sacramental life. But other parts of the law are quite flexible. I'm not suggesting that you break the law, but if you slip up and don't get a detail right with respect to another type of law, it might not be that serious. It won't affect the validity of anything.

To be adequate for the body, our skeleton needs to grow. To be adequate for the church, the law needs to grow. Canon law is not static. It evolves as a result of the experience of the church. We need a balance and a distinction between stability and rigidity. If our bones become too rigid, they break easily.

That's what happened with the 1917 Code of Canon Law. Keep in mind, we had no codified law in the church for a very long time, until 1917. We had, to be sure, lots of laws, but no codified law. Almost as soon as the Code was promulgated, however, the world and the church went through the most rapid period of change history had ever witnessed. And very quickly, the law was no longer adequate. We forget that on the same day in 1959 Pope St. John XXIII announced the Second Vatican Council, he also announced a new canon law. But he wisely decided to wait until the council had finished its work before starting work on a codification of church law. Why? Because law needs to follow theology, and we needed to see what was going to emerge from the Second Vatican Council to determine how the law should follow. And not surprisingly, since it was finally promulgated in 1983, the Code of Canon Law has changed multiple times.

Delineating Everyone's Rights and Obligations

So we need canon law to be stable, but not brittle. It gives structure to an organization. It stabilizes. It gives a human and organizational framework. If the law didn't tell you as pastors, "Here is what is expected of you," people might have wildly divergent understandings of what your role is. And if you didn't have law to say, "This is what it is," you could be pulled—if you're not already—from pillar to post, trying to figure out what you're supposed to do.

Not only does the law give you structure but it also governs how individuals relate to a larger group. How, for example, the members of a parish deal with the parish at large. It's not like a shareholder-driven corporation where everybody gets a vote. Still, the law gives structure to a parish so it can function.

The law also prescribes how one group relates to other groups within the church. We want everyone, of course, to work toward the common good. But we have to be careful that one group doesn't interpret the common good as its own personal agenda. That can easily happen at the parish level. And if you don't have structure around how your organizations function, you can have a situation where, for example, the athletic association is dictating how the rest of the parish functions.

To reiterate, you need to have structures in place at your parish that determine how one organization relates to another and how each organization relates to the parish as a whole. Canon law also exists to protect rights and to spell out obligations. We don't have rights in the church because they're in the Code of Canon Law. It's because rights are in the Code of Canon Law that we have the ability to defend them.

The 1983 Code went much further than ever before in delineating the rights and obligations of everyone in a church. There's a section on the rights and responsibilities of the clergy, for example, and another on the rights and responsibilities of the lay Christian faithful. Some rights are human rights codified within the Code of Canon Law. These include the right to one's good name and reputation. Because it's delineated in the Code, if someone within the church, within that organization, violates that right, I can make a claim. I can defend myself because the law has codified that right.

Some rights are ecclesial, that is, by virtue of your baptism you have the right to have the word of God preached to you. You have a right to the sacraments. And those are because of your baptism, not because it's in the Code. But if someone were to deny you a sacrament without cause, you'd have a hard time defending that right if it wasn't codified, if it wasn't written into the law.

Some rights are ecclesiastical by virtue of the office an individual holds. In your role as pastor, you have certain rights and faculties that come with that office. And they cannot be taken away at whim. A bishop cannot say, "I heard about that homily you preached last week. I'm taking away your preaching faculties." You're a pastor and under canon law you have a right to preach. If the bishop doesn't want you preaching anymore, what can he do? He can remove you as pastor. And there's a process for that, as well, to ensure the church doesn't violate your rights.

It's really about balancing individual rights with the common good. The fact is, I have a right, according to the Code of Canon Law, to make my needs and my personal opinions known to those in authority. There might be times when I choose not to exercise that right because I recognize it's not for the common good (for instance, if my speaking out, which is my right, might undermine the well-being of the larger group). My right didn't disappear. I'm just choosing not to exercise it.

I'd like to also point out that a set of principles was established to revise the Code of Canon Law. And one of those principles is that the law is to make clear the difference between external and internal forums. Law governs the external forum, that is, the external dimensions of life. There may be perfect consistency between what one should do morally and what one should do legally. But in the end, the law is going to deal with the legal and not the moral dimension. And be careful not to impose one on the other. Let me give you an example. In a marriage tribunal case, I must look at the grounds on which the validity of a marriage is being contested. And that means putting aside my moral judgments about the life of one or the other parties. Only if that person's moral failings impacted the marriage within the scope of which the case is being tried are they relevant. I can't just say, "This is a very bad person and I'm therefore going to find the marriage invalid." I have to carefully weigh the legal grounds for doing that. I can't mix internal and external forums.

By the same token, you can look at any of the canons and ask, "What value are we trying to protect with this canon, and what action does it provide for us to do that?"

Affirming the Church as Community

With that as background, let's move to the impact of canon law on parish and pastor, starting with the definition of a parish we find in canon 515:

> A parish is a certain community of the Christian faithful stably constituted in a particular church, whose pastoral care is entrusted to a pastor *(parochus)* as its proper pastor *(pastor)* [shepherd] under the authority of the diocesan bishop.

Each phrase needs to be teased out a bit for a fuller understanding. Let's start with "community of the Christian faithful." The original 1917 Code of Canon Law defined a parish as a territorial region within a diocese that had a church to which a pastor was assigned. So, it's a much more institutional notion of parish than we know today. A modern-day parish, according to canon 515, is a "definite community of the Christian faithful," so we sort of flipped the definition around. And that means we have to flip everything else that goes with it. If the pastor is the one entrusted with the parish, then everything he does is for the good of the community. Under the 1917 Code, we thought of the parish as a benefice—a means of financial support. No priest could be ordained without having a benefice, a named source of income. But in the United States we didn't have benefices. So the understanding was that your benefice was the good of the diocese in which you were ordained.

According to canon 515, the parish is also "established on a stable basis." It is thus presumed to continue its existence unless there's a reason for it to be reconfigured. It's stable.

As for the phrase "within a particular church," we don't entertain a congregational understanding of *parish* in the Catholic Church. We are always part of something larger than what we see before us. Indeed, the parish is larger because of its connection to the diocese and its bishop. And through the bishop, the parish and the diocese are larger because he is their connection to the universal church. We really have to work against a congregational understanding of the parish, especially in this country where we're so driven by individualism. We have to work hard at making those connections.

As we're seeing, the difference between the 1917 institutional model and the 1983 community model of the parish is more than just terminology. It's conceptual and attitudinal. The 1917 Code cast the church as a perfect society—an institution that maintains within itself everything it needs to achieve its ends. Now, with the benefit of Vatican II, we talk about the church as the *people of God*. We've shifted from perfect society to a much more biblically based notion. Put another way, we've moved from institutional to communal.

Pastor as Parish Shepherd

As our next step toward better understanding canon law, let's change the focus from parish to pastor. And begin by asking a fundamental question: What is a pastor?

Actually, that definition needs to embrace the notion of parish—a community of people. If you examine what canon law says about your role as pastor, the language makes little sense outside the notion of community. The pastor exists for the sake of the parish community; it's what gives meaning to the role and office of pastor. Pope Francis, in one of his talks, said a priest should smell like sheep. He wasn't being literal, of course, but rather making the point you should be so intertwined with your community that when he looks at you he doesn't see just you, he sees your parish. It's the biblical notion of pastor as shepherd in the name of Christ. Pastoral service clearly takes precedence over the notion of benefice. So when you take possession of your parish—and we still use that language in the Code—think of it less in terms of "It's become my property" as "I've become its shepherd." You're putting your arms around the parish, not putting the parish in your back pocket.

In terms of your actual responsibilities, here's what canon 519 says:

> The pastor *(parochus)* [parish priest] is the proper pastor . . . of the parish entrusted to him, exercising the pastoral care of the community committed to him under the authority of the diocesan bishop in whose ministry of Christ he has been called to share, so that for that same community he carries out the functions of teaching, sanctifying, and governing, also with the cooperation of other presbyters or deacons and with the assistance of lay members of the Christian faithful, according to the norm of law.

An important takeaway from this canon is that you are never alone in carrying out your responsibilities. Others within the church are called on to share the pastoral role with you, including parish priests, deacons, laity, and religious. They assist you in fulfilling your responsibilities. The fact that you don't bear the full weight doesn't mean, of course, you can simply relinquish all responsibility. In terms of *teaching*, you have a primary responsibility to see that the word of God is conveyed to all your parishioners, and that they are instructed in Christian doctrine. *Sanctifying* means presiding over the Eucharist, ensuring it's at the center of the parish assembly and that the faithful participate in the liturgy and devoutly receive the sacraments.

Ruling, or *governing*, gets a little more complicated. The administrative responsibilities assigned by law to the pastor are many and varied. One of the most important, which I'd like to touch on, is presiding over the parish pastoral council and parish finance council in order to receive the consultation necessary for the fulfillment of your pastoral role.

In other words, both serve in advisory capacities to you. Sometimes people who sit on these councils feel diminished when you remind them they're an advisory—not a deliberative—body. True, you are the ultimate decision maker, but decision making must be thought of as a process that involves researching, evaluating the information, developing options, recommending a course of action, and implementing it. That's the continuum of decision making—and the councils are involved in each step of the process. Suffice it to say if you use your pastoral and finance councils in that broad range of decision making, they will invariably see there's great meaning to the notion of being an advisory body. You need to know what your diocesan norms are on these councils (they should be available to you), as well as what the finance council functions are in your diocese.

Another aspect of governing that's entrusted to you is financial administration. When you are appointed pastor, you become the administrator of the parish. As background, the parish has a legal identity separate from its members and from the pastor. It's similar to a corporation, whose legal identity is independent of its stockholders, board, and CEO. In legal parlance, that identity is known as a juridic person. Juridic persons come into being in the church either *ipso jure*, by the law itself, or by a decree of competent authority. In the case of a parish, the law makes it a juridic person. As a juridic person, the parish has certain legal rights.

One of those legal rights is to acquire and use church property. How does the parish acquire property? There are multiple ways. The most common is through the freewill offerings of parishioners on Sunday morning. Other ways are solicited contributions—essentially fund-raising and special collections—and taxation, the assessment of which the bishop imposes on the juridic persons under his jurisdiction, including parishes. In other words, he has the right to tax in order to support the work of the diocese. However, it is not an unfettered right. He can only impose a tax that is moderate, proportional to income, and approved by the presbyteral council.

As a pastor you need to be knowledgeable about what property the parish possesses. Where are its assets held? Who is monitoring long-term investments? What are the property lines? What does the civil law say about cemeteries and do those laws apply to my parish cemetery? You do not have to be an expert in real estate, investments, or law, but you do need to have the awareness required of a good steward of the parish property.

Your Administrative Responsibilities

Under canon law, you have some very specific responsibilities as administrator of your parish. First, you must "exercise vigilance so that the goods entrusted to [your] care are in no way lost or damaged" (c. 1284 §2). This means you need to keep a close eye on your bank accounts or statements. You may well have someone in your parish in a part- or full-time bookkeeping role. But it will come as no surprise to you that some people, given the opportunity, will take financial advantage of the parish. So you need to be vigilant by knowing what's in those parish accounts. You should also exercise vigilance about property in your care by making sure you have the proper insurance coverage. You may think it's wonderful that you have an open-door policy where anybody can come in and use the parish facilities when they want. It *is* wonderful until somebody gets injured and you get sued. You need to be aware of who's allowed to use parish property, and when, under your current insurance coverage. And if outside groups are using your premises, you should make sure they have their own insurance coverage.

Second, you should make sure that the goods entrusted to your care are safe, even under civil law. So, if property is given to you as a trust, you need to preserve it as a trust. Be aware that civil law will respect your role as the trustee.

Third—and this is one of your most important responsibilities—you need to ensure that any stipulations of donors are honored and secured. For example, Mary may give $10,000 for scholarships at your school. This act of generosity puts the onus on you to keep accurate records. Don't trust it to memory. Too much can happen. You need to document the fact that Mary gave X dollars for scholarships to the parish school. And you need to know *how* she gave it. For example, did she stipulate that the principal was to remain stable and the income generated was to be used for scholarships? The best advice I can give is document, document, document.

Fourth, you need to keep accurate records of income and expenditures. This includes drawing up an account of your administration at the end of each year. You are also required to prepare budgets and annual financial reports by the norms of your diocese. Moreover, it is important to share the financial condition of the parish with your parishioners. The more candid you are with them, the more they will believe and support you when you seek their assistance.

Finally, be aware that while you, as pastor, are the administrator of the juridic person, you may not enter into any legal process, any litigation, without the permission of the diocesan bishop. It is your job to know what your legal limits are. Check your diocesan regulations for how to seek the bishop's permission if you are drawn into litigation.

There are two types of administration under your purview: ordinary and extraordinary. Ordinary administration includes everyday tasks like paying the bills and making payroll. Administration is extraordinary by virtue of the act (like putting a new roof on the parish) or its cost. Be aware, however, that extraordinary administration can differ from one parish to the next. Paving the parking lot may be considered ordinary administration in one parish because it has the income to handle it comfortably. In a less affluent parish it may be considered extraordinary administration.

Don't make an educated guess at which category an expenditure or project in your parish falls into. You should check with your diocesan finance office on what acts are extraordinary—therefore requiring the permission of the bishop—and which are ordinary, usually meaning you can proceed on your own.

Canon Law as a Bridge, Not a Burden

I'd like to leave you with this thought: Don't think of canon law as a burden, or as something you pull off the shelf and throw at someone when you have a point to make, as in "it's expressly allowed" or "not allowed," under the Code of Canon Law. Rather, think of it as a bridge that gets you from one place to another. You'll find within canon law basic principles and a framework for fulfilling your responsibilities as pastor. But canon law does not provide an answer to every issue you're going to face. You should be looking for assistance—and wise counsel—from other collaborators, ordained and lay, including your staff and parish councils.

Finally, rely on the ever-present guidance of the Holy Spirit. I can't emphasize that enough. If you've got a big decision to make, don't go first to the Code of Canon Law. Go first to that place of silence and contemplation and ask for the guidance of the Holy Spirit. Then see if you can integrate canon law into your pastoral ministry in a way that helps you make good judgments on behalf of the community entrusted to your care.

Getting a Handle on Human Resources

Carol Fowler

The pastor of a parish has the fundamental responsibility to serve as a leader, preacher, teacher, presider, and person of God for his people. Under this umbrella comes the role of human resources administrator and, more specifically, being the leader of a diverse group of staff and volunteers in order to implement the mission of the church within the parish and link it to the larger mission of the diocese. That's why knowing some of the administrative practicalities of leading a staff is so critical to your job as pastor.

Are you aware, for example, of the questions you're forbidden to ask during a job interview? Do you know what steps you need to take before firing someone, or why a cash arrangement with an employee is a bad idea all around? Or why performance reviews and job descriptions are two things you can't live without?

Human resources, or HR, takes in an incredible range of personnel issues, from recruiting and hiring to supervising and coaching to payroll and records keeping. While there's no way a single chapter could hope to adequately cover all of these, I'd like to draw your attention to a number of areas under the HR umbrella that you should have at least a fundamental knowledge of to be an effective administrator for your parish.

First, I'd like to dwell on four basic terms you need to know. The first two describe how we classify employees. The second two are on how we classify employers. For our purposes, there are two types of employees: exempt and nonexempt. Exempt from what, you might ask? The answer is overtime pay. There are two requirements for being defined as "exempt." The first is the nature of the job description, the parameters of which are described in the Fair Labor Standards Act and subsequent rules from the US Department of Labor. The second is the minimum amount of pay that a person must receive to be considered exempt from overtime, even when the job description requirements are met.

It's helpful to know at this point what types of employees are exempt and nonexempt. Exempt are defined as those whose positions require a specialized course of study, usually through a four-year college degree. They include teachers, principals, site administrators, business managers, pastors, associate pastors, qualified professional lay ministers, and others having supervisory authority. As you may already know, what we sometimes do in the church is give a staff member a better title because we can't afford to give him or her a raise. For example, we may start calling the bookkeeper a business manager, even though this person still functions as bookkeeper. That doesn't necessarily mean he or she meets the requirement of exempt. By the same token, if your parish secretary is still a secretary, it doesn't make him or her exempt if you start using the title administrative assistant.

It really has to do with the job description. And most administrative assistants, secretaries, bookkeepers, office clerks, librarians, and maintenance workers are classified as nonexempt. When employees are nonexempt, you have to keep track of their hours, requiring some kind of time sheet records that are signed by both you and the employees and kept for three years. Most important, you need to pay nonexempt employees for every hour they work, and if they work more than forty hours in a single week you must pay them time and a half. It's all spelled out in the Fair Labor Standards Act.

What you must remember is that 100 percent of proof for an overtime claim filed by a disgruntled employee belongs to the employer, not the employee. And the only way you can provide that proof is to rigorously keep time sheets that are signed by both parties. You may assign responsibility for signing these time sheets to someone else with supervisory authority, such as your business manager.

Now for the two types of employers. The first is an "at-will" employer, defined as one who reserves the right under state laws to terminate any employee for any reason, with or without notice, with or without cause, providing such termination is not discriminatory. Most state governments give employers that right in their constitutions. And while at-will employers might seem to have a huge advantage, there's a bigger potential downside. It stems from the fact that if a lawsuit is brought against you as an employer, the defense attorney could use at-will employment as grounds for the client's case.

As employers in the church sector, we recognize that from time to time our legal advisers and advocates may use an at-will defense for a particular claim. However, as a pastor, you're always better off to think and act as a "just-cause" employer—the second type of employer—because it means you're more likely to do the right thing in a given situation. A just-cause employer is one who doesn't take corrective action, including termination, without having a clear, compelling, and justifiable reason. There are lots of just causes. You might run out of money, for example, and can't pay the employee. Or the individual may perform poorly or create a work environment so toxic that no one else can get work done. Regardless of the reason, we must always think of ourselves as just-cause employers, and not take action against any employee without being able to unequivocally justify it.

Beware of Job Discrimination

As employers, we're also bound by the federal government's Equal Employment Opportunity Act. And that forbids discrimination in a host of areas.

We may not discriminate, for example, against people over the age of forty. People under age forty are not protected by age discrimination. So if you decide you're going to hire someone who is over the age of forty as opposed to somebody who's under that age, you cannot be accused of age discrimination. Conversely, if you hire somebody under the age of forty versus somebody over that age and their qualifications are equal, the older candidate could file a suit against you alleging age discrimination.

As a longtime HR person, I can tell you that age discrimination is the thing we fear most. And that stems from the fact that hearing officers in age discrimination cases will more often than not identify with the older people, perhaps betraying their own age bias. The onus is on you in the course of hiring someone to be able to show why that person is better suited for the job. You need to get specific about the skills or experience that makes him or her more attractive than the other candidate, and why he or she is a better fit for the culture and ecclesiology of your parish. And it can't be because of age.

Also, we cannot discriminate based on gender. The way this most commonly comes up is if we decide not to hire someone because she's twenty-seven years old, just married, and therefore likely within a year or two to have a baby and ask for maternity leave. In other words, we're not going to hire her because she may get pregnant. That's a classic example of gender discrimination. We don't discriminate against men because they're newly married and their wives may become pregnant, and we can't do it with women. For that reason, we're forbidden in the course of a job interview to ask a woman about not just age but also marital status.

Other areas where discrimination is forbidden under federal law are race, nationality, and ethnicity. Religious preference is one area, however, we are allowed to consider in the course of hiring. Under the Equal Employment Opportunity Act (1972), we can—repeat, *can*—ask candidates if they're Catholic. We have that right as a religious organization. I would suggest, though, framing your discussion this way: "If you're going to come work for us—whether you're Catholic or not—you must live according to the teachings of the Catholic Church." In this way, we're telling people who are not Catholic that they still have to support our mission, or we can't serve as their employer.

If employees are required to live according to the teachings of the Catholic Church, then how do we respond to those who don't follow these expectations? My answer is to treat them the same way we would treat someone who's been drinking on the job. Our first response shouldn't be to fire them, but to help them deal with the problem. We might say, "We want to help you, and here's the name of someone at Catholic Charities (or another reputable support group) we think you should see." In the case of a person who is divorced and remarried without an annulment, we could say, "We'd like to help you do what's necessary to straighten out your marriage with the church." That, I think, is what our stance has to be: to make clear we want to support them because we deeply value their service and don't want to lose them as employees.

The Benefits of a Personnel Handbook

To give us guidance across the many sensitive areas of HR, it's important to have a set of just and clear personnel policies. These policies should be consistent with civil law. They should be fairly and consistently applied and communicated to all employees in your parish. And they should be compiled into a readily available handbook. Many times the diocese will send you a list of personnel policies and tell you to adopt them, giving you some leeway to make changes tailored to your parish. If a handbook isn't available, work through the diocese to develop one for your parish.

What kind of policies should this handbook cover? Major areas include pay scales, job descriptions, performance reviews, work schedules, and work-at-home policies. This last item deserves some elaboration. You might arrive as a new pastor and have three of your seven staff members tell you they work at home three days a week. If you're uncomfortable with that—and you might have good reason to be—you'd have grounds to say, "That's going to change immediately. You must be at your desk during regular work hours." And to support your case you'd hopefully be able to refer them to the appropriate section of the diocesan/parish handbook on employment practices.

Other areas that might be covered under written policies include dress standards (business casual is appropriate for most parishes these days), children in the workplace (whether a parent can bring to work a sick child who can't go to school), and outside employment (it should be made clear that this employment will not infringe in any way on their full-time work with the parish).

On the subject of documentation, I can't stress enough the importance of maintaining a comprehensive file on each employee. As a new pastor you should carefully review each of those files soon after arriving. Find out, first of all, if they even exist and, if so, whether they contain job descriptions that make sense to you.

Job descriptions are a particularly effective personnel management tool. They should detail the functions, duties, responsibilities, and reporting structure of each staff position. Why is this so important? Because the job description sets a baseline for your expectations of the employee. These expectations must be crystal clear to both you and the employee to prevent any ambiguities or misunderstandings. That's why I urge you to carefully review and then renew each description with the employee upon taking over as pastor. There may be times, for example, when the description does not reflect what you perceive the job's actual responsibilities to be. In these cases, you have the right to make changes—and make them quickly. Remember, a job description is not final until you as pastor say it is.

Be aware, too, that a job description should distinguish between *basic* functions and *essential* functions. Basic functions are, as the name suggests, tasks, duties, and responsibilities that support the goals and mission of that position. Essential functions are usually narrower in scope. They are those functions that, if an employee is no longer physically or mentally able to fulfill, might disqualify him or her from holding that job. For example, a maintenance person might be required to lift fifty-pound boxes of textbooks when they arrive at the beginning of the school year. If that employee becomes permanently disabled and can no longer perform that essential function, it could be a deal breaker. I suggest you go through each job description and put an asterisk next to each function that you deem to be essential, and make those designations clear to the employee. Failure to do so could result in your having to hire more help at additional cost to the parish.

No less important than job descriptions are performance reviews. These are written appraisals of an employee's performance prepared by the pastor and conveyed privately to the employee. This is your chance to tell a staff member, "Good job, but here are some areas I think we need to work on." Performance reviews should be, for the most part, positive experiences. And there shouldn't be any surprises for employees in these reviews. That's because if there's a problem, it should have been previously communicated to the worker. Employees need both positive and negative feedback—and it should be continuous. The purpose of the performance review is to formally capture and summarize that feedback.

The rationale is clear: if you don't tell people what the problem is, they can't fix it. It must be a two-way street. And if the feedback is negative, make sure it's communicated in private to the employee. You want his or her dignity and self-respect to remain intact.

Advice on Hiring and Interviewing

Hiring is one of the most important things you will do for your parish. As the saying goes in HR circles, "The more time you spend hiring, the less time you'll spend firing." Some other words of advice are: "Don't settle." If you're in a bind to hire someone for a vacant job, don't compromise by hiring a candidate who is not fully qualified or totally satisfactory. You can always hire someone on a temporary basis, or a coordinator, until you find the right person. If that's proving to be a difficult task, you might have to review whether the salary is adequate or the job description is overwhelming for that position.

Interviewing, of course, is critical to the hiring process. It requires skills and ingenuity that may take you outside your comfort zone. You don't want to ask a question like, "Are you good at this?" and get back as a response, "No problem." As a good interviewer, you must know how to ask open-ended questions designed to draw the interviewee out and shed some light on his or her character.

There are actually two other categories of questions you should feel comfortable with. One is the behavioral question, which looks to the past. A behavioral question might be, "Describe for me a time when you had a really successful project, one where you worked with others and it produced a great outcome." You might follow up with, "What made it work?" "Who was on the team?" "What was your role?" Another good follow-up question is, "Tell me about a time you worked on a project with a group of people and it didn't work out." "What happened?" and, most important, "What did you learn from the experience?" I don't think there's ever a problem with somebody being on a project that failed. In fact, it worries me if somebody replies, "I was never part of anything that failed." That tells me he or she has never taken a risk or tried something different.

The second type of question that's used by skilled interviewers is the hypothetical question. It looks to the future and gives the job candidate a chance to solve a problem. For instance, you might say, "We've hired you as a director of religious education, but you immediately run into a group of parents so attached to the previous DRE that they won't give you a chance. They're critical of everything you do. How would you handle this challenge?" Hypothetical questions like this can reveal a lot about the person's leadership style, and you should be prepared with a list of such questions. Effective hypothetical questions often begin with, "Tell me about a time . . ." or "Think about a time . . ." or "Consider a situation in which . . ."

On the other side of the coin are the questions you must never ask during an interview. They include the age of the applicant, when he or she graduated from high school since that would give away age, marital status or family plans, nationality, if he or she has ever been arrested, and if the applicant has any disabilities.

All these caveats, however, do not preclude you from checking with references on anyone you're thinking of hiring. In fact, it's absolutely critical that you check his or her credentials through others. And you're not restricted to the references listed. You can call anybody. You can ask anybody. If he or she has worked in other parishes, call the pastor. Find out why the applicant left. Just because the previous pastor says, "It didn't work," doesn't mean it won't work for you.

A further word of caution when considering a candidate's credentials: be wary of resumes, which tend to make claims that need to be checked out. Be skeptical if someone claims to have an MBA from Harvard, for example. Call Harvard and find out. People are forever staking claim to degrees and accomplishments that are exaggerations, if not outright lies. It's important to know this in advance, because how can you trust someone with the parish money or other valuable assets if you can't trust him or her to tell the truth?

Compensation Considerations

In the field of compensation, most dioceses have guidelines that cover their parishes. This can be very helpful to you from the standpoint of being able to tap into their information base. For instance, you might learn what the average salary of a parish secretary is in your deanery, and thus get a better handle on what you should be paying. Put another way, what would this person make if he or she didn't work for you?

One of the things you must take into account when making compensation decisions, of course, is the financial means of your parish. Since the buck stops with you as pastor, it's your responsibility to meet the payroll. Repeat—you must always be able to meet the payroll. You can't hand an employee a check on Friday and say, "Please don't cash it until Tuesday when the Sunday collection has cleared the bank." If you're having trouble meeting the payroll, you need to immediately seek help from the diocese.

A word on volunteers and compensation. The church does not pay volunteers—*period*. Even if you say to them, "I'm not really paying you, I'm just giving you a little $5 gift for every time you taught CCD," that

could be construed by the government as dodging minimum wage requirements. If you want to give volunteers $25 gift cards at Christmas
or recognize them with a dinner or plaques, that's fine. But be careful
of anything else that has the appearance of compensation.

Nor should there be cash arrangements outside the payroll system
for any full- or part-time employee. You sometimes hear of a parish cook
or housekeeper being paid in cash. Why is that a bad practice? For one
thing, cash payments make you liable for state and federal penalties for
failing to withhold and submit income taxes on a quarterly basis. Second, it's bad for employees. Since cash payments do not count toward
pension or Social Security benefits, they can leave employees destitute
in their retirement years. The law is clear: no cash payments. All lay
employees, as well as priests and religious, must be paid through the
regular employee payroll. For religious staff (who have taken a vow of
poverty), however, no taxes are withheld and no W-2 form is generated.

Centralized Benefits

Employee benefits are usually administered centrally by the diocese.
And each diocese, by virtue of the contracts they negotiate, will have
requirements governing access to those benefits: With health insurance,
for example, those arrangements will specify how many hours a day or
days a week an employee must work to qualify. As a parish priest, you
can't change that. You have to abide by the diocesan rules governing
benefits.

The diocese also sets the ground rules for most other benefits, including your parish's pension plan. It can be either the traditional defined
benefit plan, or the increasingly popular defined contribution plans,
like 401(k) or 403(b). Many dioceses have moved to defined contribution plans. Other centrally administered employee benefits include
worker's compensation, family and medical leave, and unemployment
compensation. Paid-leave benefits include holidays and vacation, sick
leave, personal time, family and medical leave, and jury duty.

And while it's not a benefit in the classic sense, I feel as a church
we should allow our employees, particularly those in ministerial positions, time to attend an annual retreat. To be meaningful, it should be
a formal-type retreat at an off-site location. You can even take money
from your professional development fund to pay for it. Look at it this

way: it's important for you as head of your parish to foster the spiritual and professional development of your staff, and an annual retreat is a powerful vehicle for achieving that.

Finessing Terminations

Perhaps the most sensitive of your HR duties is terminating an employee relationship. It's useful to know that there are two types of resignations. One is a voluntary resignation, where an employee leaves of his or her own volition due to retirement, moving to another job, or a personal move to another city or state. Even though these terminations are usually on friendly terms, they still require thorough documentation. In short, you need the resignation in writing. A verbal resignation is valid and legal, but I would follow up with a registered letter that same day stating that you have accepted the person's resignation. That way it's legal and binding. And if no one else was present when the verbal resignation was delivered, I would immediately tell somebody—your business manager, associate pastor, somebody on your staff—so that you have a witness in case issues surface later on.

An exit interview should be conducted when employees resign. If they're leaving voluntarily, you'll normally have no problems getting their cooperation. It's helpful for you to ask questions like, "What worked well for you while you were here?" and the corollary, "What didn't work so well?" And you shouldn't miss the opportunity to ask, "What advice would you give me as pastor to make this a better parish?"

The second type of resignation is involuntary. While this scenario can often prove difficult for a pastor, it's not an unpastoral thing to terminate someone's employment. Sometimes it's the most pastoral thing you can do for the sake of the entire parish. The reason could be consistently poor employee performance, or perhaps the parish no longer has the budget for that position, or it's reorganizing.

Involuntary terminations can involve a host of issues—including severance, unemployment compensation, benefits, outplacement, and due process—so documentation is essential here too. Another sage piece of advice is when you terminate someone, don't do it by yourself. Have your associate pastor or business manager with you, or someone from the diocese who has been through this before. Notice should be given humanely and quickly.

Some situations warrant immediate discharge. But most terminations for performance reasons should be preceded by warnings that spell out what the problem is, what changes are required, and the consequences if they don't occur. If the termination escalates into a legal matter, you may be required to confirm that you explained to the employee the nature of the problem on more than one occasion. Just as important, that you gave the individual adequate opportunities to correct or improve performance through coaching, classes, or other remedial programs. It's important that *you* feel good that you did everything you could to avoid firing the employee. Which brings us back to the importance of performance reviews, as discussed earlier.

Anytime you have a situation that looks like it could result in a discharge, it may be helpful to get your diocese involved. They typically have a human resources professional who can assist you in achieving an outcome that is fair to both the employee and the church, and that can be defended if legally challenged.

A Helping Hand

What I've given you in this chapter is merely an entrée to the kinds of HR issues and responsibilities you must grapple with as administrative head of your parish. While the tasks may seem daunting, you can take some comfort in drawing upon an established network of professionals for guidance and support. Aside from your diocese, there's the Leadership Roundtable. This nonprofit organization of business leaders is committed to helping pastors and parishes adopt best practices in not just the field of HR but also in fiscal management, governance, and fund-raising. Another resource is the Villanova Center for Church Management and Business Ethics, which offers a variety of learning programs for new pastors. And the National Association of Church Personnel Administration, NACPA, is a good resource to know about.

Finally, I'd like to express my admiration for the tireless work you do day after day in your parish. Your taking the time to read this chapter (and, perhaps, refer to it in the future) speaks volumes of your desire to become the best pastor you possibly can be for the people you serve.

Molding Your Staff into a Pastoral Leadership Team

Dennis M. Corcoran

I recently worked with a pastor who expressed his frustration to me one day over a member of his leadership team. It seemed the pastor couldn't understand why the team member hadn't given him an important report he was expecting. To make matters worse, the pastor was leaving for vacation in less than twenty-four hours. When I asked if the staff member knew about the deadline, the pastor became even more riled and said, "I shouldn't have to tell him something so obvious!"

The pastor's predicament made me think of Patrick Lencioni's Amazing Parish initiative. Lencioni defined three disciplines needed for the success of any leader as part of a cohesive leadership team: create clarity, reinforce clarity, overcommunicate clarity. I reminded the frustrated pastor that one's expectations cannot be met unless they are communicated clearly.

This begs the point: What is the point of a leadership team? If we are guided by the Christian concept of the Body of Christ having many parts, and if we look at Jesus' methodology of calling apostles to share in leadership, it becomes clear that a collaborative style of leadership is pivotal to Christian management. No one person, other than Jesus himself, can embody what's needed to lead a parish. As a result, every pastor should call forth people who can help him minister and lead parishioners, as Christ would. Before we jump to forms and styles of a pastoral leadership team, though, let's look at some coveted characteristics of its members.

The Need to Be Relational

Heading up the list is that all leaders within a parish need to be *relational* and they need to love people. The days are long gone when the church could afford to hire employees who simply didn't like working and interacting with others. Which brings to mind the story of a new parish team member who tells this wise old pastor how parishioners should be instructed to make an appointment before coming in, lest these constant distractions keep him and other team members from getting their ministry work done. Without skipping a beat, the pastor responded, "My friend, these distractions *are* your ministry."

The first question a pastor must ask when hiring a parish leader is, "Is this person relational?" Let me be clear here what I'm *not* saying. People confuse relation-ability with personality type. I am not saying that everyone in parish leadership needs to be an extrovert. On the contrary, there needs to be different personality types to generate team synergy. I don't think it's stereotyping to say that many finance people tend to be on the introverted side. Yet I've met many leadership team members who head up finance and possess a sense of humor, speak affably to others, and get along well with all members of the leadership team. They may be introverted, but they're also analytical, process-oriented, *and* relational.

I realize any attempt to define "relational" is very subjective. There are many nuances on which pastors, who are not trained in human resources, can get tangled up. The best advice I can give to a pastor on this matter is not just to wonder if the prospective team member is relational to him but to think of the "difficult" parishioners in the parish and ask himself, would they leave an encounter with this person having a warm and comfortable feeling? I don't think it's unrealistic to say that when someone interacts with a leader in the church they expect it to be similar to what they believe an encounter with Christ would be. Put another way, if there's one thing everyone who reads the Gospel would agree on, it's that Jesus was highly relational.

A Willingness to Change

Another desirable characteristic for a member of a parish leadership team is an appreciation for lifelong learning. We have a lot of "experts" in parish life who don't understand there is always room for improvement, for adopting best practices that exist both within and outside the walls of the church. To be sure, complacency is never a good trait for a leadership team member. Far too many ministries in Catholic parishes are being done today the same as they were before the internet, smartphones, and social media. If team members aren't always looking for inventive new ways to improve their ability to minister and relate to God's people, then they're not going to be effective parish leaders. Too many leadership team members resort to the excuse, "This is the way we've always done it." They need to open their eyes and realize our world is changing at the most rapid pace in history, and that a team satisfied with doing the identical thing month after month, year after year, is going to fail miserably at attracting the next generation of the faithful.

As a result of the financial straits of so many parishes today, pastors need to be flexible and, at times, "creative" when forming a leadership team. I don't know of too many parishes able to fill all positions on that team with full-time paid employees. Many must be filled with what I call "dedicated volunteers." These are parishioners who have proven to be committed leaders and who are willing to take on some or all of the responsibilities of a paid employee—but without the check. For some parishes this may be the only option for rounding out a leadership team.

Which areas of ministry can benefit from the advice and counsel of a leadership team member? I suggest the traditional ones of Word, Worship, Service and Community, and Leadership. (I encourage parishes to use the more contemporary nomenclature of "We Learn," "We Pray," "We Serve and Celebrate," and "We Lead," respectively.) Providing this level of leadership coverage may not happen overnight. Like most improvements in the church, it will take time and persistence on the part of many people. As if finding the most qualified team members isn't hard enough, getting them to then work together may be even more challenging for a pastor. That feat means fostering three qualities on the part of all members: trust, accountability, and a willingness to find healthy ways to disagree with each other and yet still be supportive.

Spotting Trouble in Advance

A few years ago I was working with a parish on a pastoral plan. I asked the pastoral team to develop goals and objectives for two things they would be working on in the coming year, paying specific attention to what they thought success would look like in those areas. One of the members of the leadership team resisted immediately. The pastor and I met with her and tried to assure her this was a growth exercise for everyone on the team, and we would both be willing to assist her with this task. She insisted that the task itself wasn't the issue; it was that *doing* the task represented work she considered more appropriate for a corporate setting and therefore outside the purview of the Catholic Church. Nonetheless, she reluctantly agreed to work on a plan for her ministry, and each team member was given training and assistance to fill out the sample forms to complete the task. When the day came for all to share their plans, the other four members of the team offered up three to four pages of thoughtful work. The resistant staff member, however, had less than a page of objectives, citing things like "building the kingdom of God" and "bringing parishioners to Christ" as the measure of success. While there was nothing wrong theoretically with these answers, they were not precisely what the pastor had wanted. One by one the team tried to steer the obstinate staff member in a more constructive direction. It was meant to be a healthy exercise, an opportunity to build trust and support among all members. The team could have emerged stronger as a result of sharing differing perspectives and opinions, not to mention setting guidelines for accountability. Instead, the team member said she felt attacked from all sides and stormed out of the meeting.

That evening the pastor explained to me that this individual had shown relational issues from the beginning. She drew the fewest number of volunteers from the parish when petitioning for help with projects and could be quite rigid when it came to rules and procedures. She was also known to give the silent treatment to team members with whom she disagreed. In short, she was a disruptive and divisive force who on several occasions had forced the pastor to put pastoral planning on hold in order to deal with her objections.

Before addressing how to deal with such an individual, let me point out that people who struggle with relational issues also tend to struggle with trust, accountability, and the capacity to handle disagreements in a healthy manner. They often seek to vilify those with whom they disagree. In order for these nonrelational people to feel any connection to others, there has to be someone else or some other group they can direct their ire against. This, of course, puts the pastor in a difficult position since a successful leadership team depends on forging healthy relationships across the board. Sadly, the church has a history of attracting more than its share of people who don't "play nice in the sandbox," and pastors need to be aware of this legacy when considering members for parish leadership roles.

Patrick Lencioni addresses this area of vetting in his Amazing Parish work by making a distinction between smart and healthy. Not only do the two need to go together, but Lencioni points out that "healthy" is the magnifier of "smart." While his focus is mainly on smart and healthy organizations, I believe the principles also apply to individuals. People can possess great levels of expertise, talent, and giftedness, but if they can't work with others, can't function without creating drama and confusion, then they will never be useful players on a leadership team.

The Art of Team Building

Many pastors ask me for the secret of dealing with difficult team members. Trust me, there is no secret. Every team member can be difficult at times, just like every leader and pastor. We all have our issues and every now and then they can get in the way of effective pastoral ministry. Success lies in knowing how to wisely and thoughtfully manage and resolve those issues.

For many years I was involved in marriage preparation ministry. I would always start by telling the couple before me, "Two imperfect individuals are being married by an imperfect priest in an imperfect church within an imperfect world. Any questions?" The goal of a good marriage is not to seek perfection, lest you set yourself up for failure. The magic of team building with imperfect people lies in recognizing their imperfections and still being able to work successfully with them. In this way, the relationship becomes stronger over time. The imperfections can in effect act like glue for the team. Who knew the paschal mystery has implications for parish management!

This is particularly good advice when building a team from scratch or adding new members. Every pastor or administrator needs to be diligent and thorough during the hiring process. Be sure to have a search committee with people who have already been a successful part of your team. Like-minded individuals tend to attract others of the same ilk. Check references. Call people you respect who can lead you to worthy candidates. The consequences of not doing your homework can be profound. I know of a new pastor who added a minister to his team without bothering to check with her previous employer. After six months, he called me for advice on how to deal with the manifold problems she was now causing. I took the initiative to call her last two pastors and they both told me they had let her go because she wasn't able to connect with other team members or parishioners. When I asked her new pastor why he hadn't researched her more thoroughly, he told me he'd been very busy and thought her resume spoke for itself. "She's been working for the church for twenty-five years," he argued. "Shouldn't that be enough?" Lesson learned!

Orientation Period

The first year of service for any new team member should be devoted to orientation and evaluation. They need to be informed at the very beginning that they will receive a lot of information and feedback to quickly bring them up to speed and ensure they are clear about their responsibilities. To repeat Patrick Lencioni's formula for success: after you build a cohesive team, it's all about clarity, clarity, and more clarity. For each new hire there should be three-, six-, and twelve-month evaluations during the first year where both team member and pastor can have a candid and open exchange. As part of this evaluation, the pastor should collect feedback about the member from other team members and administrative assistants, as well as from parishioners. That feedback should be balanced—both positive and constructive—and it should be delivered at a meeting that is scheduled in advance.

I should point out that employees in Catholic parishes are generally unaccustomed to getting constructive feedback. They are more used to being "called on the carpet" to hear about problems or issues that have spun out of control. This amounts to unhealthy and unproductive team management, however, with lack of trust often rearing its head as a divisive issue. What's clear in hindsight is that if the problem had been addressed earlier, in the team building phase, it could have been leveraged to strengthen the relationship, rather than tear it apart.

Returning for a moment to my marriage ministry metaphor, if a husband and wife are accustomed to asking each other every month, "What can I do to be a better spouse in this relationship?" issues get dealt with in a way that is nonconfrontational and less dramatic, as opposed to screaming at each other when they simply can't take it anymore. The former helps unite and strengthen the team while the latter acts like a knife and cuts it apart. All members of the leadership team need and deserve annual, nonconfrontational, and constructive evaluations. The pastor might even take the opportunity to ask team members, "What's one thing I can do to be a better pastor?"

How Teams Learn to Click

Before you can evaluate anyone fairly, however, clear expectations need to be communicated and shared at the beginning of every year. Each team member—for that matter, each parish employee—needs a job description. If they already exist, you should consider adding *work flows*. Job descriptions tell *what* the employees do for the organization, while work flows tell *how* they do it. Good work flows may take a year for the team members to complete by thoroughly documenting all the ways their responsibilities are carried out. If a leadership team has never done an annual plan, the best way to start is to have members update their job descriptions so that they accurately represent their roles. These should be agreed upon by the pastor and/or supervisor.

As part of the team-building process, I ask each team member to look inside his or her ministry to identify two areas to target in the coming year. For example, the "We Learn" team member might identify RCIA and family-based religious education as his two projects. This member, as well as all others, should be very specific about how they intend to carry out their plans—the work flow I previously mentioned—and how their progress and success will be measured. Why are these important? Because by spelling out these two areas they are increasing the chances they will be able to connect with members of other teams who are in a position to help them. For example, let's say the "We Learn" member develops under his RCIA initiative a program to reach out to non-Catholic spouses of parishioners. Unveiling his specific plans and measures (i.e., the goal is to add five new church members) at a parish staff meeting one day, he catches the attention of a member of the "We Pray" team, who informs him that she's aware of at least three or four members of her ministry who have non-Catholic spouses, and is willing to help with the outreach. Voilà! A connection is made—one that would never have occurred if the pastor hadn't insisted on the preparation of work flows and measures by his staff members, and if they hadn't been shared with others on the leadership team.

Some pastors might question how you get team members to work together when each is so tightly involved in one's own two initiatives. Well, that collaborative spirit should already be ingrained in each member since that is how relational people behave. They don't need training to find ways to work together since it's already built into their DNA. Nonetheless, it should be clearly communicated to members at the outset.

I can't emphasize enough that every activity we've discussed—the job descriptions, the two initiatives, the work flows, and evaluations—needs to be documented on paper. This way, if someone is terminated, retires, or resigns, the replacement doesn't have to start from scratch; he or she can hit the ground running thanks to the supportive documents.

Achieving the Right Chemistry

I want to share some final thoughts on staffing and team management. Many dioceses have set up policies for pastors, forbidding contracts with employees in order to guard against lawsuits should a termination take place. While I applaud the human resources departments for consciousness-raising with regard to the Fair Labor Standards Act, I must point out that as a result of offering no commitment or security to employees, we are losing many talented people to other nonprofit organizations. I encourage bishops to examine this issue to try to find a way to commit without leaving the church vulnerable. At the same time, I encourage pastors to find ways to express their appreciation to their most treasured employees. It's interesting to note that in recent surveys, employees ranked "appreciation and affirmation from my superior" as high as "bonus and salary increase" as ways they would like to be recognized for a job well done.[1]

It makes sense, too, to avoid hiring parishioners. I'm not saying never hire them, but understand that if the relationship falters, you may lose not just an employee but also a parishioner. Worse yet, if that disaffected parishioner decides to hang around, they could start bad-mouthing you to the church and the community, putting you on the defensive. What can be said with certainty is that hiring a parishioner is always a gamble. Some of the best and worst employees I've experienced in parishes have been parishioners. When the relationship is good, it's usually very good, but when it's bad (as the expression goes), it's horrible. The best advice

I can give is to go with your gut when making a final determination. If you have any doubts, wisdom dictates passing on the parishioner as an employee. And if you're a new pastor who has inherited employees who are parishioners, I suggest having a cup of coffee with them and, with a big smile, ask, "What are you going to do as a parishioner if you find you can't work with me as your employer?" This may sound a little bold and presumptuous, but it serves to identify the elephant in the room and can only be beneficial in the long run.

I also urge you not to tolerate triangulation among team members. The rule has to be that if a team member has an issue with another member, including the pastor, no matter how big or small, he or she needs to come to *you*—not another team member behind your back. Not only is the latter unhealthy, childish, and unprofessional but also it erodes trust across the team and complicates issues under discussion. Unfortunately, it's also typical of the nonconfrontational church culture that's evolved, where people are conditioned to be friendly and to avoid conflict with others. Pastors often exacerbate this behavior because they too are inept at dealing with conflict. There is a way, however, to be assertive without offending others. It involves the pastor selecting and handing out to each staff member a small token or object, like a Nerf ball, with his or her name on it. If a member becomes upset with someone over an incident small or large, he or she simply leaves the Nerf ball on the desk of that individual to signal that they need to talk about a pressing matter. This opens the door to a constructive conversation that can ultimately build on relationships, making the entire team stronger in the long run.

Based on my experience working with parishes, I would say the optimal organizational chemistry is achieved when the parish leadership team is focused on animating, delegating, and implementing ministries within the parish; when the pastoral advisory council is deciding what the priorities of those ministries need to be; and when the finance council is figuring out how to pay for it.

How will you know if you have a strong, effective, and successful leadership team? You will know when productivity, morale, energy, and trust are high, and drama, distractions, conflict, and whispering in the hallways are minimal. It's that simple. Or that complex.

Endnote

1. *Trends in Employee Recognition* (Scottsdale, AZ: WorldatWork, 2013), https://www.worldatwork.org/adimLink?id=72689.

Frameworks and Tools That Drive the Parish Finance Council

Jim Lundholm-Eades

The parish finance council is just one part of a comprehensive system the Catholic Church has put in place to help the pastor and community discern the will of God for his people. The pastor, the pastoral council, the finance council, and, indeed, the whole parish community seek to do the will of God through the relationships they form. To that end, members of the parish finance council reflectively address parish financial matters and draw on their talents to offer competent and prayerfully considered counsel to the pastor about the fiscal affairs of the parish.

"Best practice" finance councils use consistent frames of reference to guide what they do and a pragmatic set of tools to get the work done. The following three frameworks highlight the thinking behind their work.

Framework One: *Missio* and *Communio*

Parish finance councils create for members an experience of *communio* focused on *missio*. *Communio* is the experience of the Lord in the gathering of the faithful to do God's will. *Missio* is the great mandate given to the church by Jesus to carry his good news to the world. In Catholic tradition, articulated so well by Pope St. John Paul II, *communio* exists for *missio* and *missio* is always carried out in the context of *communio* (*Christifideles Laici* [1988]).

Why is this important to a finance council? Because a finance council needs to remain focused on *missio* as it executes its work as an integral part of the whole parish system. Whatever the agenda of the finance council at a particular time, *missio* must remain at the heart of the conversation about parish finances in order to keep its work from being about the parish as a "business," or about money as an end in itself. In short, *missio* puts the work of the finance council in perspective.[1]

Framework Two: Fundamental Relationships

Canon law holds that each parish *must* have a finance council (c. 537) but only *may* have a pastoral council (c. 536). Many bishops, however, make pastoral councils mandatory through either policy or decree (c. 536). The pastoral council helps the pastor choose pastoral priorities of the parish. Members prayerfully consider all the options in the light of what they know about the community and its needs and make recommendations on pastoral priorities and how to put them into action. Those items are often identified in practical terms as liturgical rhythm and practice, sacramental and catechetical programs, evangelization initiatives, pastoral outreach, and resources and preferences in staffing levels or positions. The finance council thereupon takes the work of the pastoral council and expresses it in terms of a responsible budget that meets guidelines set by the local bishop on diocesan policy, other guidelines that may be set by the pastor, and civil and canon law.

The key to the success of both pastoral and finance councils is the quality of the relationships between them, as well as with the pastor. This dialogue within the *communio* is one key means by which the will of God emerges and is made clear, and so the pastor adopts a stance of prayerful attentiveness to what these counselors are saying to him in their deliberations and recommendations.

Framework Three: Governance and Management

The work of a finance council falls much more into the governance frame than it does management, but it crosses both to varying degrees. The pastor, whom the finance council advises, governs the parish and part of his responsibility is to ensure its proper financial management. Bottom line, it is the pastor, not the finance council, who is accountable for governing the finances of the parish and for daily financial management.

However, the real value of the finance council lies in giving counsel to the pastor more in his governance role than in his management role. Governance here refers to giving the parish a "big picture" perspective in terms of direction (where are we going?), vision (how will we know when we've arrived?), action steps (how will we get there?), and perpetuity (stewardship of the gifts given by God to the parish and its people). Management refers to being organized and operating within the clear boundaries and direction set at the governance level in the parish. As a result, the council's core focus—expressed as agenda items—should be more geared to ensuring the perpetuity of the parish than on daily operational matters. Be aware that while the council may get involved in both, its central job is helping with the financial aspects of governance of the parish rather than fiscal operations. In most parishes, daily financial management resides with a staff hired for that purpose, an independent service contracted by the parish, or an office of the diocese set up to do management for parishes.

Pragmatic Tools for Finance Councils

Tool One: Targeted Information

Finance council members need to be informed about the financial health of the parish. Their deliberations are mission driven and data informed. For example, they use financial reports provided by the parish on a monthly basis to monitor how well the parish is meeting its ongoing fiscal obligations and aligning with the budget approved by the pastor. To that end, there are five questions the pastor and every finance council member should be able to answer after reviewing the financial reports:

1. What is the current cash balance in each parish account (checking, investments, diocesan deposit, loan fund, etc.)?
2. What are the principal balances for any parish capital or operating debt obligations?
3. Can the parish meet its current operating cash obligations during the next twelve months?
4. Can the parish meet its debt obligations during the next thirty-six months?

5. What unfunded obligations do not appear in the financial reports of the parish, such as deferred maintenance projects, legal settlements to which the parish may have to contribute, capital projects under discussion, or staffing increases being prioritized, considered, or at least under discussion?

Some parishes have a staff person prepare the answers to these questions each month in the form of what is known as a *dashboard report*. This is a summary of key information in a brief report (often a page or less) that goes to every finance council member before each meeting. Parish dashboard reports can become quite sophisticated, which is great if everyone is able to understand them. But if the report includes measures like financial ratios (i.e., common ratio, debt ratio), it may be necessary to help the pastor and other members interpret them.

Tool Two: Member Expertise and Competencies

Most finance councils consist of between seven and twelve parishioners who have expertise relevant to the group's work. Local diocesan guidelines often govern the composition and size of the finance council. For example, it is common for a bishop to promulgate a policy that finance councils consist primarily of adult parishioners who are active in the parish, while those who are not parishioners must be both Catholic and recommended by their own pastor. Some diocesan policies also state that finance council members need to have expertise in fiscal management, such as banking and finance, insurance, accounting, law, property management, and business administration. Some parishes even have a checklist of competencies they distribute to the parish when seeking finance council members to show the current range of expertise on the panel and identify gaps that need to be filled. The checklist is a great tool for other parish consultative groups to use when looking for new members to fill their ranks.

The pastor is always a member of the finance council. What's more, the council can only meet with his knowledge and approval since it's the relationship between him and the finance council (as well as with the pastoral council) that makes up the consultative system designed by the church.

Most policies and guidelines prescribe term limits for finance council members, often three years with the opportunity for a one-term renewal. If a finance council does not have term limits, the pastor usually establishes a staggered three-year schedule for term expirations so they don't all occur at the same time (see the *Catholic Standards for Excellence*, published by Leadership Roundtable at http://www .theleadershiproundtable.org/sfx/default.asp).

Tool Three: Focused, Agenda-Driven Meetings

The work of the finance council has a predictable rhythm that enables the pastor and the chair of the finance council to establish an annual cycle of meeting agendas for the group. Indeed, an essential tool for staying focused is the meeting agenda. Every finance council meeting needs an agenda and because of the predictability of the rhythm of its work, finance council agendas can be planned well in advance.

There are often two categories of agenda items: (1) those relating to the month-to-month monitoring of parish fiscal performance, and (2) those relating to the longer term financial health of the parish. The matter of *when* these items are addressed depends in part on the timing of the pastoral council carrying out its duties of helping the pastor identify priorities and changes to programs, staffing levels, and more. Introducing any kind of capital works project or significant maintenance project also impacts the timing of the finance council agenda.

Ongoing monitoring of the financial health of the parish should be part of most finance council meetings. Agenda items might include:

- A comparison of actual revenue and expenses with budgeted revenue and expenses, and recommendations for adjustments to both in order to keep the parish on track with its budget. The budget report with the actual and budget numbers might also include percentage variance and dollar variance columns. Members of the finance council who have expertise can provide insight into whether these variances are significant.

- A review of the monthly cash flow (also known as "profit and loss") statement for both bottom-line performance and for any significant change or extraordinary expenses or revenues that might improve or otherwise change the financial position of the parish. Finance council members with professional experience in this area can provide insights and suggest key questions members need to discuss.

- Assurance that any taxes due for unrelated business income are paid on time to the IRS.

Agenda items that relate to the long-term financial health of the parish include:

- Evaluating the revenue side of parish fiscal performance against projections and making recommendations about revenue assumptions for the next two to three years.
- Reviewing revenues and expenses related to the new and emerging priorities and activities the pastoral council is considering recommending, and turning the findings of that review into budget assumptions for use if these proposals are adopted.
- Making recommendations for assumptions about revenue and expenses that will guide budgeting for the next fiscal year.
- Preparing a budget proposal for the pastor to consider approving that is based on the priorities the pastor has approved in consultation with the pastoral council.
- Recommending a responsible budget that meets all guidelines established by the bishop and the pastor. This is normally an annual budget, but many parishes are beginning to make biannual budgets, especially when capital debt is involved.
- Reviewing audit/review reports, especially any management letters, for deficiencies related to financial controls as well as to capacity to service debt.
- Standing by the pastor (sometimes literally) when he shares the final approved budget with the parish, or when difficult news about parish finances needs to be shared. Proposing a system by which all parishioners get financial information and have the opportunity to discuss it.
- Recommending updates to parish financial control policy and procedure as operating conditions, law, and diocesan policy change.
- Recommending staffing structure for the temporal administration of the parish.

On occasion there is a need for specific items to appear on the finance council agenda, such as:

- Examining the mission of the parish with the help of the pastoral council so that finance council members can identify the values and priorities that need to be expressed in the budget they are developing.

- Holding a spiritual retreat—including catechesis on discernment—so that finance council members can better participate in decisions and consultation in the context of Catholic teaching and tradition.

- Developing a fraud policy. Over 85 percent of dioceses reported financial fraud over the last five years, underscoring the need to address this crucial area. A fraud policy is a standard protocol to follow—such as a mandatory call to police—when fraud (or theft) is uncovered. More than 93 percent of fraud cases uncovered in dioceses over the last five years were in fact reported to the police and, of those cases, 91 percent were on a scale that made an insurance claim necessary.[2]

Tool Four: Investment in Time and Preparation

Any pastor inviting people to join a finance council should make his expectations explicit up front. They will invariably include the requirement that members do their "homework" before meetings so they arrive well prepared (e.g., having digested the current financial report). Finance council members are also expected to invest in developing a robust prayer life that includes asking guidance of the Holy Spirit, and participation in the liturgical life of the parish. Furthermore, they need to invest the time in getting to know other pastoral council members (meeting somebody for coffee is a great tactic) in order to understand their perspective on the parish's pastoral plan. Such encounters also enable finance council members to learn more about their own role in the parish. One of the best ways to broaden their horizons, of course, is to *read*. The documents listed in the resources section at the end of this chapter, which speak to the work of the parish finance council, are an excellent starting point.

Conclusion: Drawing Boundaries

Some matters are clearly outside the purview of the finance council. For example, the consultative forum for developing a pastoral plan for the parish is the responsibility of the pastoral council (the finance council applies its expertise to the pastoral plan). Nor should the finance council

- do performance evaluations of staff members or make decisions about hiring or terminating employees;
- make financial decisions for the pastor;
- recommend policy or procedures that ignore diocesan policy, particular law established by the bishop, civil law, or canon law;
- sign contracts on behalf of the parish;
- make recommendations that are against Catholic teaching.

Notwithstanding these natural boundaries, the parish finance council enjoys a broad range of responsibilities that are integral to the pastoral plan and the mission of the church. Through their ongoing partnership with the pastor and pastoral council, the dedicated members of the finance council play a vital counseling role that ultimately leaves a bold mark on both the temporal and spiritual work of the parish.

Endnotes

1. See Brenda Hermann and James T. Gaston, *Build a Life-Giving Parish: The Gift of Counsel in the Modern World* (Liguori, MO: Liguori Publications, 2010).

2. See Chuck Zech, "Challenges and Opportunities Associated with Parish Finances," Villanova University, Center for Church Management and Business Ethics, https://www1.villanova.edu/content/dam/villanova/VSB/centers/church/21conference/Parish%20Finances%20-%20Chuck%20Zech.pdf.

Resources for Further Reading

A Framework for Diocesan Internal Controls

USCCB Committee on Budget and Finance, "Diocesan Internal Controls: A Framework," http://www.usccb.org/about/financial-reporting/diocesan-internal-controls-framework.cfm.

A Sample of a Diocesan Guide for Parish Finance Councils

Diocese of Bismarck, "Parish Finance Council's Role and Responsibilities," http://bismarckdiocese.com/documents/Finance/ParishFinanceCouncilsRolesandResponsibilities.pdf.

A Sample of a Guide for Parish Finance Councils

St. John Eudes Catholic Church, "Guidelines for Parish Finance Councils," http://www.sjeparish.net/forms/financecouncilguidelines.pdf.

Easy Reading on Canon Law Related to Parish Finance Councils

Cathy Caridi, "Canon Law and Parish Councils," *Canon Law Made Easy*, http://canonlawmadeeasy.com/2014/10/02/canon-law-and-parish-councils/.

Nonprofit Financial Management Resources

American Institute of CPAs, "Not-for-Profit Resources," http://www.aicpa.org/InterestAreas/NotForProfit/Resources/Pages/default.aspx.

On Consultation in Catholic Parishes Specific to Parish Finance Councils

Brenda Hermann and James T. Gaston, *Build a Life-Giving Parish: The Gift of Counsel in the Modern World* (Liguori, MO: Liguori Publications, 2010).

On Communio *and* Missio *and the Role of the Laity*

John Paul II, *Christifideles Laici*, December 30, 1988, Libreria Editrice Vaticana, http://w2.vatican.va/content/john-paul-ii/en/apost_exhor tations/documents/hf_jp-ii_exh_30121988_christifideles-laici.html.

Standards for Finance Councils

Leadership Roundtable, *Catholic Standards for Excellence*, http://www .theleadershiproundtable.org/sfx/default.asp.

The Pastoral Council and Consultative Leadership

Mark F. Fischer and Paul Spellman

Pastoral councils are a success story within the US Catholic Church because they enable pastors to be good shepherds. Council members help a pastor to make decisions based on trustworthy information and thorough reflection. And that allows the pastor, like a good shepherd, to lead his flock to green pastures and flowing waters. He knows and confidently consults with council members. They return that trust.

In our home, the Archdiocese of Los Angeles, some pastors say that councils are the "eyes and ears" of the parish because no pastor wants to be the last in his parish to know about an issue. Council members often bring things to the pastor's attention that he's unaware of, gladly relying on members to keep him apprised of what is happening in the pews. Still other pastors view the council as a volunteer parish staff. They say, "I am so happy to have a group of leaders who will plan my anniversary celebration, organize the parish picnic, and make sure that parking is arranged for Ash Wednesday, Christmas, and Easter!" The most consultative pastors invite their councils to study a parish issue and recommend the best response. They see the council members as pastoral planners. But among these three views of the pastoral council tension can arise, as we shall see.

Statistics help us gauge the success of pastoral councils. For example, these bodies currently have a presence in fully 85 percent of US parishes. Another sign of success is their support by bishops. A 2003 survey by the US Conference of Catholic Bishops reports that 65 percent of dioceses mandate the establishment of pastoral councils. In addition,

43 percent of US dioceses employ an office or staff person to support councils. Unlike finance councils, pastoral councils are not mandated by canon law. The US bishops' strong support for such councils indicates the value they place on them.[1]

The number of pastoral councils has grown in the half century since Vatican II, and our understanding of them has grown as well. In this chapter, we will first sketch the evolution of councils (their origin is somewhat obscure and they have not always been as well understood as they are today). Next, we will consider what councils imply about the pastoral role of parish priests (the principle of consultative leadership has consequences for the way that priests should relate to the parish). Finally, we will discuss what pastors and council members ought to assume about the pastoral council (the church's official teaching implies various expectations about the relationship between the two; meeting these expectations can take us a long way toward better councils).

Recently, a nearby pastor made a decision after consulting his council. The decision was not only a good one but also boosted the council's morale. The pastor was fairly new to the parish and wanted to establish a food distribution program. He had seen it work very well at his previous parish. Thinking that the distribution program was a brilliant idea, he presented it to the council almost as a "done deal." It turned out not to be. When he proposed his idea, council members informed him of a similar project that had failed miserably only a few years earlier. They explained why it had failed, and the pastor listened closely. He thereupon realized why his idea might have been good at another parish but would have created problems in his new home. With the council's help, he scaled the distribution proposal back. In its place, he and the council planned a food pantry. Council members were pleased their voices were heard.

Defining the Role of Pastoral Councils

Unfortunately, not every council today sees itself as a body of consultants to whom the pastor turns for better understanding and thorough consideration of an issue. Judging from the literature of the 1970s, the earliest parish councils were participative bodies that would give parishioners an active role in parish governance by initiating programs, sharing responsibility, and fostering cooperation. Early authors said that councils expressed democracy in the church. They enfranchised the laity, which hitherto had played merely a passive role. Serving the church's apostolate was their spiritual core. Early councils, in short, viewed themselves as representatives of the parish, but their relationship to the pastor as the parish's official representative was unclear.[2] This lack of clarity has persisted in some councils to this day.

One source of confusion has been a dispute about the proper foundation of councils in the documents of Vatican II. The dispute is complicated but worth following. The earliest parish councils referred to the 1965 Decree on the Apostolate of Lay People as their foundation. The decree recommended councils to assist the lay apostolate of service in the world and did not even use the term "pastoral" to describe such councils. The laity decree, however, was the only Vatican II document to refer to councils at the parish level. It said that such councils "can see to the coordination of the various lay associations and undertakings" (26).[3] This led many to conclude that the duty of parish councils is to "coordinate," that is, to lead. People assumed that such councils would lead parish ministries. Such an assumption can at times obscure the leadership of the pastor.

It was the Vatican II Decree on the Pastoral Office of Bishops in the Church (not the laity decree) that recommended "pastoral" councils. The duty of such councils, it said, is to investigate, reflect upon, and recommend conclusions about pastoral matters (27). But such councils were envisioned in the bishops decree only at the diocesan level. It spoke of *diocesan* pastoral councils, not *parish* pastoral councils. The earliest parish councils did not cite the bishops decree because it had not mentioned them. In 1973, a Vatican Congregation issued to bishops a letter that extended the diocesan pastoral council idea to parishes.[4] So the Vatican II decree on bishops, even if it does not mention pastoral councils at the parish level, is the proper foundation for them.

In 1983, Pope St. John Paul II issued the revised Code of Canon Law. Canon 537 recommended parish "pastoral" councils, the kind of council discussed in the bishops decree. It did not even mention the lay apostolate councils discussed in the laity decree. The affirmation of the "pastoral" council in 1983 confirmed that such councils serve the pastor by means of a threefold task—investigating, reflecting, and recommending conclusions. They are not meant to coordinate parish ministries. Canon 537 stated that the parish pastoral council has a consultative vote. It is not a leadership body separate from the pastor.

When councils understand themselves as a leadership body distinct from the pastor, serious problems can arise. A new pastor in his first parish told us that the pastoral council had a lot of good ideas, but there were differences of opinion on some key issues. The council chair finally said to the other members, "Let's vote on it, and then tell Father what he needs to do." At that point the new pastor gently reminded them that he wanted to hear each person's opinion, and that a vote was not necessary. Each voice was to be heard and respected. Based on what he heard from each person, he said that he wanted to make the decision. This surprised some of the members, but the pastor needed to make it clear that their responsibility was to advise him concerning pastoral matters, not to dictate a course of action.

The revised Code of Canon Law helped to make it clear that the pastoral council serves the apostolate of the pastor—the apostolate of parish leadership. The word "pastoral" does not refer to a prayerful style, to a sacred (as distinct from secular) subject matter, or to the use of spiritual discernment (in contrast to parliamentary procedure). It refers rather to the ministry of the pastor. *He consults the pastoral council in order to make wise decisions on the parish's behalf.*

The Evolution of Councils

The 1983 publication of the revised Code confirmed the Vatican II teaching about pastoral councils with their threefold task. Despite that, some practitioners today still view the council as a body that coordinates parish ministries. Its members represent the ministries, according to this view, and the council sets policy for them. Because the council members belong to the ministries they represent, participating in their activities, they are thought to monitor them and ensure that they follow the council's policies. The "pastoral council of ministries" understood itself primarily as a way to organize and coordinate the parish.[5] But in retrospect, it tended to blur the distinction between the consultative role of the council and the executive role of the pastor.

By the 1990s, the theory of councils underwent another shift. Pastoral councils came to be seen as planning bodies. From this viewpoint, the pastor consults by inviting his council to develop plans for the parish. When he accepts the plans and implements them, they become parish policy. Councils ought to plan in a comprehensive way, according to this view, and experts defined various areas for planning: evangelization, worship, community, stewardship, and so forth.[6]

The comprehensive planning model rightly acknowledged the role of the pastor as the parish's official representative. Eventually, however, it produced a backlash. Some pastors argued that the pastoral council should *not* be the primary planning body in the parish.[7] They said that planning—defined as an activity tightly focused on parish programs and activities—is too narrow. The concerns of the parish should be broader. Some pastors expressed a hunger for a wide-ranging dialogue with councils about society, culture, and the signs of the times. They did not want to do pastoral planning, especially as it had been defined for them by experts and officials.

Despite this criticism, pastoral planning continues to be a shorthand term for the proper work of councils. It well expresses the task of investigating, reflecting, and proposing courses of action. Planning is a broad term and does not necessarily entail a commitment to a specific planning methodology.[8] Pastors may ask councils to plan in a variety of ways and about any practical subject matter. Understanding the council as a planning body does not limit the freedom of pastors to consult as they see fit.

No pastor wants to be told how to consult his council. After all, he probably knows his parish better than any outside expert. He knows how to draw upon the wisdom of the council members with their many years of active involvement in the parish. Some council members, however, may have a narrow view of consultation. Some may feel that they are there "to represent their ministry." Too often a council member may assume, "I am here representing the school, and if this issue does not affect the school, I will not say anything." This can hinder the consultation. It is important to note that while council members are most likely involved in parish ministries, they are not on the council to represent those ministries. They are there to participate in parish planning so that the decisions the pastor makes are best for all concerned.

The Consultative Leader

Having traced the origin of the pastoral council from the 1965 decree on bishops, and seen some of the forms that councils have taken up until now, we need to consider the implications for the pastor. The church's teaching about councils implies that today's pastor should be a consultative leader. The church has highly recommended pastoral councils. The good pastor is the one who knows how to consult them.

There was a time when the pastoral council was viewed as a body that would free the pastor from mundane chores so that he could better serve his people. With a good parish council, Bernard Lyons wrote in 1971, "The priest no longer needs to be the corporate executive, no more the bookkeeper, fund-raiser, and employer."[9] Lyons speculated that the council would take these chores off the pastor's back. Today we know better. Pastoral councils are not meant to do chores that pastors would prefer to avoid. On the contrary, councils help pastors to make decisions that only the pastor can make (i.e., decisions on behalf of the parish) and to base them on wise consultation.

As the leader of the parish, the pastor has responsibility for its budget and employees, but he is no mere bureaucrat. On the contrary, the bishop has entrusted the parish to him precisely because the practical workings of the parish—its administration, finance, and human relations—are also occasions for pastoral leadership. We no longer regard the pastor as leading exclusively in spiritual matters while the council reigns supreme in administration (separate from pastoral ministry). No, the pastor exercises leadership in the broadest sense. The celebration of the liturgy and the sacraments is only the first of a priest's distinctive duties, which include parish administration.[10] He leads with the help of trusted consultants.

The church's teaching about pastoral councils, without explicitly defining the concept of consultative leadership, clearly implies it. Consultation is integral to the leadership of the pastor who invites his council to investigate, reflect, and draw conclusions. This vision of the council, with its implications for pastoral leadership, was not just taught at Vatican II. It was confirmed in seven separate Vatican documents from 1966 to 2004.[11] They imply that the good pastor knows how to guide an investigation. He decides when the council has sufficiently reflected. He judges whether to accept its recommendations or not.

Deciding how much consultation is "enough" may be the most difficult decision for the pastor, especially the one who is new to the parish. Unfortunately some council members may feel that the previous pastor ignored them, or simply smiled and nodded. Now that the new pastor is here, they may feel that they are "making up for lost time." They use the council meetings to tell the new pastor all that had gone on in the past, hoping that he will give in to all of their requests. Some council members will tell new pastors, "Oh, Father, you are a breath of fresh air to this parish." In fact, what they mean is, "The former pastor is gone, and this is my chance to express all of my concerns, whether they are related to the topic at hand or not!" It is important for new pastors to hear what each person has to say, but council members have to stay on topic. All should have a chance to express their opinions, but the pastor has to say when he has heard enough.

Consultative leadership is so important that its absence can harm a parish. When pastors do not guide the council's investigations, council meetings may drift into irrelevance. Without a pastor to judge that a council has reflected sufficiently, discussions may become interminable and morale may fall. And whenever a pastor refuses to bring closure to a topic by accepting the council's recommendations or explaining why he cannot, he deprives the council of its greatest satisfaction: having him accept and implement the council's conclusions. When pastors refuse to consult or engage with councils, they reject the church's own teaching.[12]

What Pastors Should Expect

Official teaching about pastoral councils is sparse. The church documents do not specify *how* the pastor should consult. We have to read between the lines to see there are five implications:

The *first* (and most important) implication is that the pastor consults the council. That may seem self-evident, but its consequences are not always obvious. If the pastor consults, it means that he has expectations. He is looking for good advice. He is investing his time in the council with the hope that the council will help him be a better pastor.

The *second* implication is that the pastor seeks a specific kind of advice. He wants advice that is based on thorough investigation. He wants the results of the investigation to be well considered. And he is looking for a conclusion, a recommendation about how to act. The council has succeeded when its study is so complete, its reflections so thorough, that the pastor accepts the recommendations and implements them. He recognizes that they will help him serve his people better.

The task of the council—investigation, reflection, and conclusion— has a *third* implication: what a pastoral council is *not*. It is not a volunteer parish staff with whom the pastor shares his workload. The church's documents are clear that the council is a consultative body, not an unpaid parish staff or pastoral team. (The documents imply a distinction between consultative role and executive role.) To an even lesser degree is the council a coordinating body that ensures the compliance of other ministers. Some have tried to popularize the pastoral council as a "council of ministries" that coordinates parish groups by setting policy (as ratified by the pastor) and by disseminating that policy.[13] But that is an executive role that belongs to the pastor and his staff. The pastor should consult the council, but its members are not policy-makers in their own right or the overseers of staff and volunteers.

If the pastor expects to benefit from the council, he needs to know the members and trust them. That is a *fourth* implication. Knowledge and trust do not come immediately. So it is wise for a new pastor—or a seasoned pastor who has newly come to a parish—to begin by consulting the council in general terms. For example, he can ask the council to define the top ten needs of the parish and put them in order of importance. Or he can ask the council to craft a parish mission statement that identifies its most important goals and correlates them with the parish budget. Or he can ask the council to study what other parishes have done and consider applying the practice locally.[14] By consulting the council about a very general topic, the newly arrived pastor can give the council a meaningful task and give himself time to get to know and trust the members.

This has a *fifth* implication, namely, that the parish has a reliable way of selecting council members. The most important criterion for council membership is the ability to accomplish its official task of investigating, reflecting, and reaching a wise conclusion. This is more important than the question of where members live, or what language they speak, or what politics they espouse. Pastors should compare the parish's usual method for selecting council members with the methods recommended in diocesan or archdiocesan guidelines. They may actually be better. If the council is "successful"—that is, if the council's recommendations are so wise and sound that pastors accept and implement them—there should be no shortage of parishioners wanting to serve on the council. Many parishioners will want to be part of a group that is building up the parish and contributing to the pastor's leadership.

There is a direct connection between council morale and the ability to attract talented and well-motivated parishioners. When morale is high, the word spreads throughout the parish. To be sure, many parishioners are unaware that their parish has a pastoral council. Many come to Mass, grab their bulletin and doughnut on the way out, and pay little attention to the parish's inner workings. Fortunately there are exceptions. Many parishioners are involved in parish ministries as servants who have the gift of service. They are happy to have met other parishioners who are in the same ministry or other ministries. This helps them to connect to their faith community and to feel that they are a part of the church. Ministry fulfills them, and they are happy that the parish has an ordained leader who consults them. When parishioners see a pastor acting on the basis of consultation, they are more likely to want to serve on the council.

In order to attract strong members to the council, the parish community should know that the voices of council members are being heard. The pastor may not agree with every council member, and he may feel that a decision he is making is not popular with certain people. But he must do what is best for the parish and the surrounding community. When council members feel that their voices are being heard—even when the pastor does not agree with everything—morale increases and word gets out that good things are happening.

In short, the official documents of the church do not explicitly state how a pastor ought to consult. But they imply it. They imply that he is seeking wise council, based on research and reflection. They imply that the pastor wants prudent counselors who can do the council's intellectual and spiritual work. The council is a consultative body, which implies that it is not the coordinator of ministries. If the pastor is to successfully consult, he has to give himself time to get to know and trust the members, so that he can accept the council's recommendations and implement them. That makes a council a winner. And that is what attracts people to the council ministry.

Conclusion

In this chapter we have considered the Catholic Church's official teaching about pastoral councils. The church does not recommend a pastoral council to free pastors from the practical work of leading the parish. Councils were not intended to do the jobs that pastors dislike. The specific role of the council is to help the pastor make wise decisions. He consults his council because he knows that he faces urgent questions and he wants to decide these questions in a way that will strengthen the Body of Christ.

We saw that the consultative ministry makes demands on both pastor and council. The pastor, for his part, has to lead the consultation. He has to know the limits of his knowledge and be willing to ask his council members to study the issues, to reflect with him about them, and to offer him wise counsel. The council members, for their part, have to be willing to do what the church expects them to do. Under the pastor's direction, they have to study the issues that the parish confronts, to bring the results of their investigation to serious reflection, and to recommend a sound conclusion. If the pastor cannot accept the council's conclusion, he should explain his objections and invite the council to take them into account. His aim, as shepherd of the parish, is to hold the community together, and that includes the members of the council.

The church's teaching implies a common understanding of the relationship between the parish member and the pastor who leads in the spirit of the Good Shepherd. Good shepherds consult their people because they want to serve them. They seek the wisdom that builds up the community. Council members want to be consulted so they can express and unfold the wisdom of Christ. Ultimately, the Holy Spirit unifies pastor and council members when they develop plans that the pastor wants to implement.

Endnotes

1. Charles E. Zech, Mary L. Gautier, Robert J. Miller, and Mary E. Bendyna, *Best Practices of Catholic Pastoral and Finance Councils* (Huntington, IN: Our Sunday Visitor, 2010), 23. The statistics on the number of councils, dioceses that mandate them, and offices that support them are based on responses to a 2003 survey conducted by the Committee on the Laity of the US Conference of Catholic Bishops.

2. Mark F. Fischer, *Pastoral Councils in Today's Catholic Parish* (Mystic, CT: Twenty-Third Publications/Bayard, 2001). See chap. 8, "The Earliest Parish Councils," 68–78.

3. Quotations of Vatican II documents are taken from Austin Flannery, ed., *Vatican Council II: Constitutions, Decrees, Declarations; The Basic Sixteen Documents* (Collegeville, MN: Liturgical Press, 2014).

4. Congregation for the Clergy, "Patterns in Local Pastoral Councils," Circular letter to the world's bishops, *Omnes Christifideles*, January 25, 1973, *Origins* 3, no. 12 (September 13, 1973): 186–90.

5. The "council of ministries" is a term coined by Thomas Sweetser and Carol Wisniewski Holden in *Leadership in a Successful Parish* (San Francisco: Harper and Row, 1987), 126. A similar idea is articulated in William J. Rademacher with Marliss Rogers in *The New Practical Guide for Parish Councils* (Mystic, CT: Twenty-Third Publications, 1988).

6. Mary Ann Gubish and Susan Jenny with Arlene McGannon, *Revisioning the Parish Pastoral Council: A Workbook* (Mahwah, NJ: Paulist Press, 2001), defined seven planning areas, 63ff.

7. Brenda Hermann and James T. Gaston, *Build a Life-Giving Parish: The Gift of Counsel in the Modern World* (Liguori, MO: Liguori Publications, 2010), 102.

8. See, for example, Dan R. Ebener and Frederick L. Smith, *Strategic Planning: An Interactive Process for Leaders* (Mahwah, NJ: Paulist Press, 2015); and William L. Pickett, *A Concise Guide to Pastoral Planning* (Notre Dame, IN: Ave Maria Press, 2007).

9. Bernard Lyons, *Leaders for Parish Councils: A Handbook of Training Techniques* (Techny, IL: Divine Word Publications, 1971), 13.

10. Joseph Ippolito, Mark A. Latcovich, and Joyce Malyn-Smith, *In Fulfillment of Their Mission: The Duties and Tasks of a Roman Catholic Priest: An Assessment Project* (Washington, DC: National Catholic Educational Association, 2008); see "The Nine Ministerial Duties of a Catholic Priest," which include parish administration, 15–17. See also the post-synodal apostolic exhortation of Pope John Paul II, I Will Give You Shepherds: On the Formation of Priests in the Circumstances of the Present Day, *Pastores Dabo Vobis*, March 25, 1992, Libreria Editrice Vaticana, http://w2.vatican.va/content/john-paul-ii/en /apost_exhortations/documents/hf_jp-ii_exh_25031992_pastores-dabo-vobis .html. In chap. 3 on "The Spiritual Life of the Priest" (at no. 26), the Holy Father speaks of the *munus regendi* or the task of pastoral leadership.

11. These are the 1966 *Ecclesiae Sanctae I* (16); the 1971 *De Sacerdotio Ministeriali* (2.ii.3); the 1973 *Ecclesiae Imago* (204); the 1973 *Omnes Christifideles* (9); the 1983 Code of Canon Law (c. 511); the 2002 document by the Congregation for the Clergy, "The Priest, Pastor and Leader" (26); and the 2004 *Apostolorum Successores* (184). These are discussed in Mark F. Fischer, *Making Parish Councils Pastoral* (Mahwah, NJ: Paulist Press, 2010), chaps. 10–13.

12. For example, see Michael White and Tom Corcoran, *Rebuilt: Awakening the Faithful, Reaching the Lost, Making Church Matter* (Notre Dame, IN: Ave Maria Press, 2013). The authors paid a high price to enlarge their congregation when they "stopped hosting town-hall style meetings, soliciting suggestions,

or taking polls" (62). They spoke of the pastoral council only once, calling it an "unfriendly debate" (115), and isolated themselves, referring to the parish office as a "bunker" (61).

13. See endnote 5.

14. See, for example, Paul Wilkes, *Excellent Catholic Parishes: The Guide to Best Places and Practices* (Mahwah, NJ: Paulist Press, 2001).

7
Effective Parish Meetings

Peter Denio

A colleague of mine who is a pastoral associate in a suburban parish tells of the time he passed a parishioner in the hallway of the parish center. The individual offhandedly remarked, "I have the pastoral council meeting tonight, but I hate going. It's such a waste of time." After the encounter, the pastoral associate thought about how unfortunate it was to have a dedicated parishioner feel that his time and gifts were being wasted at what should be such an important gathering for the parish. Later that same day, the pastoral associate crossed paths with the pastor of the parish. As they stopped to discuss a few items of business, the memory of the exchange with the parishioner was still fresh in the associate's mind. He contemplated bringing it up, but before he could the pastor ventured, "Tonight's the pastoral council meeting, and I dread going. It feels like we never accomplish anything."

I'm sure you've been there. We all have! Maybe not specifically with regard to your pastoral council, but other groups and meetings that have prompted similar thoughts. For all the bad raps they take, though, meetings are necessary. Effective meetings can help the parish move toward a common vision articulated by the pastor and pastoral council. They can advance creative solutions to difficult and challenging pastoral problems. On the other hand, meetings all too often turn into unproductive—even detrimental—exchanges between participants, convinced their time was ill spent. Such sentiments over time can lead people to feel frustrated, burnt out, apathetic, or even helpless. And I submit that ineffective meetings can contribute to the stagnation of parish life and are a major cause of "maintenance mentality" in a majority of parishes, where the same activity is done year after year without attempting to link it to a broader vision of where the parish is headed or what should be changed to meet new pastoral challenges.

As pastor, you know that meetings run the gamut from sit-downs with pre-Cana couples to staff meetings to sessions with individuals for pastoral care or counseling, and from parish plenary sessions to diocesan committee meetings to small Christian community or prayer groups—sometimes all in one day! My goal is to identify some key principles and structures that can help pastoral leaders run tighter and more productive parish meetings. And in so doing, I'd like to focus on meetings that directly impact the goals and vision of the parish. These typically involve the parish pastoral staff, finance and pastoral councils, stewardship committee, and other ministry leadership teams.

Where Should I Spend My Limited Time?

As pastor you're used to delegating responsibilities to parish bodies that work with you toward a common vision for the parish. You also spend time ministering and interacting with those you serve. But to what degree do you give—and should you give—to each?

The simple answer is that you need to strike a balance. You may find yourself doing 80 percent direct ministry and 20 percent collaboration with parish leadership bodies and ministry leaders. If you're in the process of taking the parish toward new goals propelled by a bold new vision, then your time should probably be weighted more toward working with leadership bodies. This isn't to say that all parishioners shouldn't have access to you. But if you find it hard to focus on strategic leadership decisions required of you, then it's time to take a second look at how you're allocating your time. True, you may be the only priest in the parish or you may find a dearth of leadership talent around you. In these cases, however, the onus is even greater to transition responsibilities that don't require your gifts or authority as pastor to someone else. One "best practice" is to have two volunteer coleaders for all parish leadership positions to ensure continuity, stability, and succession.

Is This Meeting Necessary
(and if So, Do I Need to Be There)?

"Father, can I meet with you?" Even if you've grown weary of hearing that request, you need to take it seriously. The reason is clear: if you make yourself inaccessible to people in leadership roles, you run the risk of stifling the flow of information and ideas essential to creative problem solving and building a parish focused on the future.

The converse is also true. As pastor you may be invited or, if parish responsibilities are not clearly delegated, *required* to attend meetings where your presence isn't really essential. One way to excise these expendable meetings from your pastoral life is to pose a couple of fundamental questions: (1) What is the purpose of the meeting? and (2) Do I really need to be the one attending?

If the meeting has anything to do with the parish's longer range goals and vision, or with an urgent pending matter, then you probably should be present. If, on the other hand, you determine your presence is not required, you should consider delegating the responsibility to a staff or council member or parishioner. Here are some additional questions to help with that decision:

- Am I comfortable delegating responsibility to someone else?
- If I delegate, does the person have the information needed to present the item at the meeting, or do I need to spend time now or later preparing and updating them?
- Is there any information that can be sent to participants ahead of the meeting that might allow for a more informed conversation?

Remember, too, there are times when you should simply postpone a meeting due to greater priorities on your plate, or because your own personal obligations or wellness demand it. As pastor, you have the prerogative to make that call.

How to Avoid "Meeting Soup"

Patrick Lencioni, a business management consultant and Catholic layman who has donated considerable time to advising church leadership, describes how parish meetings often devolve into what he calls "meeting soup"—brimming with a hodgepodge of agenda items that are often unrelated and have varying levels of importance. For example, the replacement of folding tables and chairs for the parish recreation room may compete on the agenda with development of a program designed to lead parishioners to a greater role in evangelization. This can easily happen when there is a lack of understanding and agreement over the parish's priorities and how to structure effective meetings around them. Just as important, a way must be found to match attendees to the appropriate agenda items so that individuals are not wasting their time on matters unrelated to their parish roles and responsibilities.

Keeping Your Meetings Priority Driven

To avoid getting mired in "meeting soup," key leadership (pastoral staff, pastoral and finance council members) must have a clear understanding of the most important priority for the parish. With this as a baseline, it becomes much easier to set the agenda for targeted leadership meetings with the right people attending. I can't emphasize it enough: knowing the parish's priority is the greatest imperative for effective meetings.

How does a parish identify this priority? The pastor in consultation with the parish staff and councils, and sometimes other key groups, needs to take the lead. The priority should be set every one to three years. That's long enough to give the parish time to make substantial progress toward its vision, but short enough to create a sense of urgency.

For example, let's say a parish decides to adopt the *field hospital image of church*, as called for by Pope Francis, as its top priority over the next two to three years. As it moves toward that goal, the following criteria are important:

1. It is tightly focused on a *single priority*: becoming a *field hospital*.
2. Its work is *qualitative*: the experience of the ministries and activities will be evaluated on how well they live up to the vision of being a field hospital.
3. The job is *time-bound*: two to three years.
4. The goal is *affirmed and shared* by all in pastoral leadership. It cannot only be the pastor's vision; all those in leadership should assent and commit to it.

With this priority set, the pastor, staff, and key ministry leaders can enter into their yearly pastoral planning meeting (typically off-site; see below under meeting types) by identifying and discussing the three to five strategies best suited to lead them toward that vision for their church. A highly functioning organization with sufficient staff and resources can probably handle up to eight strategies. Parishes stretched for talent, time, and resources, however, would be well advised to start out with fewer strategies, and increase them over time.

The following three strategies might emerge at that pastoral planning meeting on the road to becoming a *field hospital* for the parish and community:

1. Identify and respond to the greatest pastoral needs (physical, social, and spiritual) in their community.
2. Emphasize the healing sacraments of reconciliation and the anointing of the sick throughout parish activities, wherever possible.
3. Increase attention to and care for the pastoral needs—physical, social, and spiritual—of those involved in sacramental preparation within the parish (First Eucharist, confirmation, RCIA, marriage preparation).

To repeat, it's critical to identify the parish's top priority and strategies. Only then can all pastoral leadership teams and councils structure their meetings with clarity.

Select the Most Appropriate Type of Meeting

In the following chart, management expert Patrick Lencioni describes the various types of meetings tailored to specific needs, along with their formats.[1]

Meeting Type	Time Required	Purpose / Format	Keys to Success
Daily check-in	5–10 minutes	Share daily schedules and activities	• Don't sit down • Keep it administrative • Don't cancel
Weekly or bimonthly staff meeting	45–90 minutes	Review weekly activities and metrics and resolve tactical obstacles and issues	• Don't set agenda until after initial reporting • Postpone strategic discussions
Ad hoc topical	2–4 hours	Discuss, analyze, brainstorm, and decide upon critical issues affecting long-term plans	• Limit to 1–2 topics • Prepare and do research ahead of meeting • Engage in good conflict
Quarterly/ off-site	1–2 days	Review strategy, landscape, trends, key personnel, team development	• Get out of parish office • Focus on work; limit social activities • Don't over-structure or overburden schedule

The Daily Check-In

A seldom-used approach to parish meetings with the potential to significantly upgrade communications is known as the daily check-in. Part of the challenge today is that ministry happens around the clock. Pastoral and administrative staffs, along with volunteers, are engaged at different and diverse times of the day and week, often resulting in miscommunication or absence of communication and collaboration.

Daily check-ins should be timed to coincide with periods of the day and week when most key ministerial and administrative leaders are present at the parish. Those might be right after daily Mass, for example, or just before lunch, or thirty minutes before the close of the parish office for the day. Experiment and explore what works best for your parish. Ideally, you should block out one time, or in some cases two times, a day for these five-to-ten-minute on-your-feet check-ins. It's my experience that so much more can be accomplished when people know there's a reserved time during which they're likely to connect with people they need to talk to. As Lencioni emphasizes, these meetings should be no longer than ten minutes—a rule that should be strictly enforced. Within this format, quick questions, updates, and scheduling matters can be effectively dispatched. Some of the greatest benefits will accrue to pastors, who will begin to see fewer interruptions in their daily schedules. The other good news is that if someone misses a check-in meeting, another is only twenty-four hours away.

The Weekly or Bimonthly Staff Meeting

This is probably the most common type of parish meeting, important because it provides an opportunity for the staff to stay informed about progress on priorities identified by the parish. Just as important, it ensures that the pastor and other key leaders are privy to the conversations and information essential to moving the parish toward its goals.

The weekly/bimonthly staff meeting serves as a problem-solving space. Ideally, information is provided to participants ahead of time, which requires some advance reading and preparation. That feature, in turn, helps to ensure wise and productive use of time when the meeting takes place. Indeed, individuals are more likely to become engaged with an issue, challenge, or matter of concern to the parish when they've already made an investment in its solution.

Be advised that the staff meeting—like each of the other meeting types—has a standard duration that should be obeyed. If a matter can't be resolved within that time frame, then an *ad hoc meeting* (see meeting types, below) should be scheduled, rather than taxing everyone's patience and brain cells by dragging it out.

For maximum effectiveness, the forty-five-to-ninety-minute weekly or bimonthly staff meeting should include the following elements:

Faith sharing. An essential aspect of any parish meeting, particularly those that involve key parish leadership, is faith sharing. This is different from the *read prayer* or *rote prayer* done in unison. It's a time where group members reflect together on their lives informed by faith.

A version of the *lectio divina* prayer style is perfect for this meditation or for other forms of faith sharing that purposely connect our lives to our faith. Why is this so important?

- It grounds the conversation and deliberations that follow to our relationship with God. Intentionally inviting the Holy Spirit into our minds and hearts changes us and has the power to change our conversations. We are able to do more and do it based on the will of God (instead of our own will) when we spend time listening to what God has to say to us *first* instead of us speaking first or, perhaps even worse, not listening at all.

- It strengthens the bond within the leadership community. Paul's image of us as the Body of Christ can only be true if we work at making it reality. We need to understand the "joys and hopes, the grief and anguish" (*Gaudium et Spes* 1) of each other if we are truly to live as St. Paul taught, "so that there may be no division in the body, but that [its members] may have the same concern for one another" (1 Cor 12:25).

- The reflection is valuable to all preachers of the parish whose responsibility it is to tend to what is happening in the parish and the wider society.[2]

A "lightning round." The next few minutes of the staff meeting should be used for brief updates on matters that can be resolved through a simple yes or no answer or an on-the-spot administrative decision. If the matter is more complex—say two ministry leaders need to connect about an upcoming night of reflection during Lent or information needs to be passed from one staff member to another regarding a conversation with a parishioner after Mass—then time should be set aside following the meeting to discuss it in greater detail. The overarching goal of this phase of the meeting is brevity, and the facilitator (and ideally all members at the meeting) need to hold participants accountable.

Developing a "scoreboard." According to Lencioni's formula for good meetings, the agenda should be set *after* the lightning round. That's correct—the agenda should not be created ahead of the meeting! This may sound counterintuitive, but the truth is that your leadership agenda should in effect already exist: *It's the priority and strategies previously identified by the parish.* In the example above, the agenda is to become a *field hospital* for the parish and the community, and to that end three concrete strategies were identified. Without clarity on where the parish is going (its vision) or how leadership plans to get there (its strategies), leadership meetings can meander between competing priorities among participants. With a vision and strategies in place, however, the pathway is clear for a productive session.

Lencioni's "scoreboard" is a great way to actually nail down the agenda. The process starts by identifying each strategy, and rating it with a color code, as follows:

- *Green* if progress is being made according to plan.
- *Yellow* if there is some delay or challenge, but work is still proceeding.
- *Red* if the item could benefit from group discussion and problem solving.

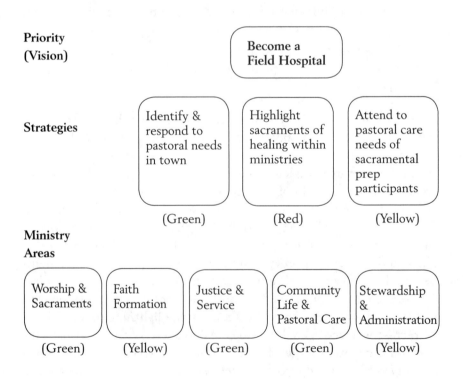

The agenda for the meeting thus becomes any strategy identified as red. Green strategies never make it to the table because they are going according to the plan. Yellow strategies become simply an update so participants are aware of any delay.

The beauty of this approach is manifold: (1) it focuses members on what they have determined is the group's priority for the parish; (2) it eliminates ancillary topics that sometimes find their way into agendas when they don't really belong there; (3) it keeps the focus of the meeting on problem solving (as it should be at a leadership meeting) and not on reporting; and (4) items that have been identified as important but not in need of problem solving are not discussed, freeing up meeting time for more pressing matters facing the parish.

The facilitator of the meeting can be anyone on the team, or the job can rotate among staff members. I have seen meetings where the pastor or the pastoral or finance council chair served quite successfully in that role. A standardized process for identifying the agenda alleviates the burden on the facilitator. This allows the facilitator to focus on his or her primary responsibilities of ensuring (1) all viewpoints are raised and discussed, (2) a decision or action is identified by the close of the conversation, and (3) there is clarity on the agreed-upon decision or action and commitment by the participants to execute it.

Each strategy has a designated monitor. At the meeting, when the scoreboard is being reviewed in order to create the agenda, each monitor is asked to identify progress on the strategy, using the color-coded system. The monitor is not the person who is solely responsible for seeing the strategy through—that rests with the entire leadership team (and likely others within the parish). Instead, the monitor is charged with being aware of and reporting on progress relevant to the strategy. Color coding, for its part, is a quick way to determine if some challenge or problem has arisen that makes it necessary to add the strategy to the agenda, subjecting it to a full discussion by the leadership team.

Returning to the example shown in the chart, the only item that belongs on the weekly or bimonthly staff meeting agenda is the one in red ("highlight sacraments of healing within ministries"). The strategy, "identify and respond to pastoral needs in town," is moving according to plan (green), so there's no need at this time to take up valuable meeting time with it. The other strategy, "attend to pastoral care needs of sacramental preparation participants," has been delayed (yellow), meaning it has not progressed according to plan, but the plan has been modified and that change is communicated to the leadership team during the scoreboard review. Therefore no further discussion or intervention is required by the leadership team.

Other items compete for attention, of course, within any parish (like those shown on the bottom line of the scoreboard example). The scoreboard process acknowledges that while parish leadership is focused on top-tier issues, the parish staff is occupied with a diversity of still-important areas (i.e., worship and sacraments, faith formation, justice and service) that often require collaboration and problem solving by the full team. If one of these areas—all green or yellow on the above chart—were to turn to red, then it too would be placed on the meeting agenda for plenary discussion.

Through this system of prioritizing agenda items, you can save countless hours of time during the year by uncluttering and streamlining parish meetings. At times a discussion item will require more in-depth treatment, but it may not require the involvement of the entire team. In these cases, the agenda item should be moved to one of the two remaining types of meetings—ad hoc topical or quarterly/off-site review (explained below).

Summary and follow-through. About ten minutes before the close of the meeting, the discussion is halted and the designated scribe reads to the group the decisions that have been made and actions to be taken. This is not a formal accounting of every discussion at the meeting. Instead, it covers such essential information as (1) the agreed-upon actions by the group to move the strategies forward, (2) who in the parish needs to know about the decisions that have been made, (3) who from the meeting will communicate this information, and (4) the time frame for communicating this information to key constituents. This review process helps to clarify and gain consensus on these areas and how the group has determined to move forward.

Summary and follow-through help to ensure that the most important topics for the parish are being discussed and communicated in a timely manner. And while the example used here was keyed to a parish staff, this approach (with some simple modifications) could be just as effective for pastoral and finance councils, commissions and ministry teams.

The Ad Hoc Topical Meeting

These two-to-four-hour meetings are limited to one or two topics that demand significant discussion. Because of their highly focused nature, ad hoc topical meetings give participants the chance to analyze and brainstorm crucial issues that impact the parish's long-term plans. They are specifically designed for key leaders and individuals responsible for or familiar with the topics under discussion. Advance preparation and research are usually required and information should usually be sent ahead of the meeting so the session can be devoted to discussion.

My experience is that weighty church items are often mistakenly assigned to weekly/bimonthly staff meetings. The result is that matters warranting in-depth discussion receive insufficient time or, even worse, no time at these sessions. That sets up a situation where decisions are either rushed or not made at all, to the detriment of the entire parish.

The Quarterly/Off-Site Review

This type of carefully planned and highly structured meeting is generally meant for pastoral and finance councils, or for annual ministry leadership planning. The format—spread over one to two days—allows sufficient time and an off-site setting conducive to extensively reviewing progress on key issues, team development, goal setting, and much more. It's important, however, not to overschedule or overburden these meetings.

If a ministry in your parish has an advisory committee, such as stewardship or worship, it should consider adopting the quarterly/off-site review format for its major get-togethers. Ministries like catechesis, which have more frequent work, might use a combination of weekly/bimonthly meetings and quarterly/off-site reviews.

Be aware too that facilitators can be a huge asset to your ad hoc topical or quarterly off-site meetings. These individuals—from either inside or outside the church—typically come with a variety of skills and knowledge sets that can significantly improve the flow, content, and clarity of meetings. In the end, they can make a difference in terms of how much participants are able to retain and accomplish.

Facilitators are an important way, in addition to choosing the right type of meeting from the ones we've just discussed, that pastors and other parish leaders can draw on "best practices" from both the ecclesial and business worlds to ensure their meetings produce the best possible outcomes in service to the church's mission.

Endnotes

1. Adapted from Patrick Lencioni, *Death by Meeting: A Leadership Fable* (San Francisco: Jossey-Bass, 2004).

2. "The preacher also needs to keep his ear to the people and to discover what it is that the faithful need to hear. A preacher has to contemplate the word, but he also has to contemplate his people" (*Evangelii Gaudium* 154).

Ten Essential Building Blocks
for Developing a Stewardship Parish

Charles E. Zech

One of the most misunderstood terms in contemporary Catholic parish life is "stewardship." For many parishioners, it is simply a synonym for fund-raising. But stewardship is much more than that. It has variously been described as

- a recognition that everything we have is really a gift from God, who asks us to return a portion in the form of our time, talent, and treasure to support God's work on earth;
- an understanding of a total way of life, a conversion of mind and heart;
- not about something we do, but about who we are, and whose we are;
- developing a need to give, rather than merely giving to a need;
- asking ourselves what we own and what owns us.

In this context, introducing stewardship into a parish is actually a spiritual activity, meant to make the parish a more spiritual place. One of the happy consequences of becoming a stewardship parish is that parishioners become more generous in providing their time, talent, and treasure.

The fact is, Catholics are not nearly as generous as Protestants in supporting their church, especially in the area of treasure. Study after study has found a remarkable pattern—US Catholics contribute about half as much to their parish as Protestants do to their congregation. The typical Catholic household contributes about 1.1 to 1.2 percent of its income to the parish, while the typical Protestant household contributes 2.2 to 2.5 percent of its income to their congregation. In dollar terms, this means that US Catholic parishes could receive another $8 billion a year in revenue if their parishioners contributed at just the same rate as their Protestant friends. I'm not talking about tithing, but just the same 2.2 to 2.5 percent of their household income.

To put it another way, each parish would see its annual revenue double! Imagine what your parish could do with twice the revenues. Think of the scandalously low salaries that we pay our lay staff. Think of the maintenance that we keep putting off year after year because we can't afford it. Think of the outreach we could do. The list goes on and on. That is what is at stake here.

For a variety of reasons many priests find it easy to preach on the time and talent aspects of stewardship but are reluctant to openly discuss the treasure component. It might be helpful for them to recall the theological basis for stewardship and to recognize that raising treasure is in itself a spiritual activity.

Theological Basis for Parish Stewardship

We're all familiar with the biblical notion of stewardship. The master has gone on a trip and charged the steward with overseeing the household in his absence. When the master returns he calls for an accounting. The lesson is that God has entrusted all creation to humankind. In doing so, God has given each of us a unique endowment of gifts. We are expected to use those gifts to further God's work on earth, and someday we too will be called to give an accounting of how we used our allotment of time, talent, and treasure.

In their 1992 pastoral *Stewardship: A Disciple's Response*, the US Catholic bishops provided the following summary of the theology of stewardship:

- Living a stewardship life is a manifestation of mature discipleship. It is a conscious decision to follow Christ no matter what the cost.

- Since it is a conversion of mind and heart, a commitment to stewardship is not expressed in a single action or even a series of actions, but in a person's entire way of life.

- Practicing stewardship can enable parishioners to change their understanding of their lives. Those who have been transformed into good stewards will recognize God as the source of all that they possess.

Spiritual Basis for Stewardship

Henri J. M. Nouwen, the noted spiritual writer, authored a short monograph, *A Spirituality of Fundraising*, in which he argues that raising treasure is first and foremost a form of ministry, an opportunity for us to announce our mission and invite others into our vision. It is also a call to conversion by inviting parishioners to experience a new way of relating to their resources. Nouwen argues that as a form of ministry, raising treasure is as spiritual as praying, giving a homily, or visiting the sick. He observes that raising treasure is a concrete way of helping the kingdom of God come about.[1]

Asking parishioners for treasure should involve more than just asking for money. It should be about inviting them into a new spiritual communion. We should tell parishioners that we don't just want their treasure. We want them to get to know us; we want them to get involved in building the community of faith; and we anticipate creating a lasting relationship with them.

Nouwen concludes that once a priest has prayerfully committed to placing his whole trust in God and has recognized that he is not raising money for himself, but rather is only concerned for the kingdom, and once he believes that we have great value to give those who commit their treasure, then he will have no trouble asking parishioners for their treasure. Moreover, his own vocation will be deepened and strengthened as a result.

Stewardship versus What We're Already Doing

Many, if not most, parishioners believe their parish is above average. As long as their needs are being met, they are reluctant to accept major changes, such as the introduction of stewardship. I ran into that problem in my parish when my pastor decided that we should become a stewardship parish and asked me to serve as chair of the newly formed parish stewardship committee. We ran into resistance not just from many parishioners but from some fellow members of the committee who viewed the introduction of stewardship as an indication that something was wrong with the parish. I tried to explain to them that while we had a very good parish, we could be better, and that becoming a stewardship parish would be a path toward becoming a *great* parish.

To help them understand the difference between a "good parish" and a "stewardship parish," I have adopted a table (see below) from Thomas Jeavons and Rebekah Basinger's book, *Growing Givers' Hearts*.[2] I argue that when parishioners are motivated by the stewardship side of the table, they become more generous givers. But beyond that, even greater opportunities for spiritual growth exist.

	What We're Already Doing	**Stewardship**
Focus and Goals	To bring people into a relationship with our parish and with the work it does in a way that makes them want to support it.	To bring people into a closer relationship with God through the experiences of giving time, talent, and treasure that we help to create by offering occasions where this giving is consciously evoked as a spiritual act and practice.
Ideal Outcomes	Parishioners make a contribution to the parish in recognition that the parish needs resources if it is to continue its work (that is, parishioners give to a need).	Parishioners are more generous in their gifts to the parish of their time, talent, and treasure because every gift becomes an occasion for and a celebration of growth in faith (that is, parishioners develop a need to give).

Philosophical and Cultural Underpinnings	The philosophical and cultural root is philanthropy, "private action for public purposes." The intent is to encourage people to feel a commitment to the "common good of the parish," and voluntarily give of their resources—material goods that they feel they own—for the benefit of others.	The philosophical and cultural root of stewardship is a commitment to personal and collective behavior that recognizes and honors God's ultimate ownership of and profound generosity in all things. The intent is to encourage people to see all resources as gifts temporarily entrusted to us to be used and shared to promote the welfare of all of God's creation.
Ultimate Objective	To provide financial (and other) support for our parish, so that it may carry out the Godly work to which we believe it has been called.	To "build the household of God" so there will be more human and spiritual, as well as material, resources to carry out the work of building the kingdom, in whatever form that work may take.

So, what are the steps in becoming a stewardship parish? I've identified ten essential building blocks that will help a parish transform itself into a stewardship parish. Some of these I consider to be "unintentional stewardship" blocks, that is, activities that a parish should be undertaking anyway (happily leading to more generous parishioners). Others could be labeled "intentional stewardship" blocks, activities that a parish would initiate only if it were trying to implement stewardship.

Ten Essential Building Blocks

1. Be a welcoming parish that works hard at building community. A basic tenet of fund-raising is that people give to people. While a parish might be able to rally parishioners to support a particular need (e.g., the organ needs to be replaced), long-term, sustained giving necessitates a sense of commitment to the community. Every parish should be working hard at building community. This is admittedly difficult in many of today's parishes, which may serve as many as two thousand to four thousand households. But it must be done. A parish needs to take every opportunity to be a welcoming, community-building center, a place where people want to come. This could include introducing small faith-sharing groups and programs such as RENEW. It might include adopting a sister parish or a refugee family. It surely includes encouraging parishioners to be welcoming toward strangers as well as embracing parish-sponsored social events such as potluck dinners, parish festivals, or athletic leagues and Boy Scouts/Girl Scouts.

2. Make the connection between spirituality and giving. The most generous givers in a parish are typically motivated by their relationship with God, not out of some sense of guilt or obligation. Stewardship needs to be introduced to parishioners as a holistic approach to spiritual renewal that challenges them to contemplate the role that money and possessions play in their lives, rather than as just another fund-raising gimmick. (The preceding table spells this out.)

3. Help parishioners to develop an attitude of abundance, not of scarcity. Implied in both the Hebrew and Christian Scriptures is a world of plenty. When God's righteousness reigns there is abundance for everyone. Unfortunately, we live in a consumerist society that views the world through a lens of scarcity, with limited resources that must be competed for. The result is a tendency for us to focus on our own survival. Selfishness and narrowly defined interests prevail.

Jesus taught that seeking first the reign of God will provide us with all that we truly need. After all, he fed the multitudes with just a few loaves and fishes. When we focus on the abundance that God has provided it becomes easier for us to become more generous givers. Supporting our parish becomes an essential element of Christian life, rather than a burden or merely a charitable act.

4. Emphasize that the parish has a mission, and that it is not merely a vendor of religious goods and services. Related to developing an attitude of abundance is ensuring that the parish is mission-centered rather than need-centered. In our consumerist society it is tempting for parishes to tailor their efforts to meeting the needs and wants of parishioners through multiple programs, rather than by addressing the common good. In a stewardship parish, every element of parish life is evaluated on the basis of how extensively it leads parishioners to a better understanding and more meaningful participation in the mission of the parish.

Related to this mind-set is how the parish leadership views the budget. It is easy for them to get caught up in the importance of meeting perceived parishioner needs when they present the budget to the parish. Instead, they need to divert attention from a consumerist sense of the budget to how the budget relates to the parish's mission and vision of where it is going and what it will become. Parishioners whose primary concern is to contribute their fair share of this year's budget won't be as generous as those who have bought into the parish's mission and vision.

5. The pastor and other parish leaders must model good stewardship. First and foremost, the pastor must be on board with the parish's stewardship effort. As noted above, many priests are uncomfortable asking their parishioners for money. But if the pastor fails to communicate that giving is important, many parishioners will deduce that it's not. And as disdainful as it may be, this message needs to be repeated throughout the year, as the Sunday readings warrant. Not necessarily the importance of contributing to the parish, but an examination of the larger issue: the role of money and possessions in each parishioner's life. Preaching on the topic of stewardship is essential to both the financial health of the parish and the spiritual health of parishioners and, to reiterate, such preaching can strengthen a priest's vocation, as well.

Second, it is imperative that the pastor and his leadership team (including the parish business manager and parish finance council) exhibit the highest standards of integrity and responsibility in managing the parish's financial assets. The most direct way to defend against the improper use of parish resources is to maintain transparency and accountability in all parish financial matters. This requires regular (more than annual) release of parish financial statements. But it also entails more.

Third, Vatican II has taught us that through baptism parishioners have not only a right but a responsibility to participate in parish decision making, including matters involving parish finances. This extends beyond merely keeping parishioners informed. It also involves consulting with them and giving them some direct input. Pope Emeritus Benedict XVI often referred to the "co-responsibility between the clergy and the laity for the welfare of the parish." Shared parish decision making leads to the development of mature stewardship on the part of parishioners.

Let me be very clear. If a pastor hopes to introduce stewardship into his parish, he and his staff must be examples of good stewardship. This not only means using good judgment in all parish financial matters but providing parishioners with the opportunity to share in financial decisions. I strongly believe that if my pastor wants me to contribute more to the parish, he better be prepared to demonstrate that the funds are being put to good use.

6. *Establish a parish stewardship committee.* While a pastor needs to be on board with the parish's stewardship effort, he need not be the only player or even the lead player. Introducing stewardship into a parish can be complex and time-consuming. It is best handled by a specially designated committee.

How should this committee be organized? Some parishes establish their stewardship committee as a subcommittee of the parish pastoral council. Others make it a subcommittee of the parish finance council. This latter approach is unsuitable, in my opinion, since it sends the message to parishioners that stewardship is only about money, which many already believe.

My recommendation is that the parish stewardship committee be established as a separate committee, on the same level, and with the same stature, as the parish pastoral and parish finance councils. This would send a strong message to parishioners concerning the high priority being accorded stewardship in the parish.

What would the parish stewardship council do? Certainly, one role would be to communicate to the parish about stewardship: what it is (a change of minds and hearts) and what it isn't (a mere fund-raising scheme), while presenting examples of good stewardship already taking place in the parish. It would also recruit and train lay "witnesses" who would speak to the parish about their own stewardship journeys. It would organize some sort of "ministry fair," an annual event in which each ministry presents itself to the parish, opening up opportunities for parishioners to not only learn more but join these important groups. And finally, the parish stewardship committee would play a major role in implementing building blocks 7, 8, 9, and 10.

7. Parishioners are expected to make a commitment. One of the major differences in the way Catholic parishes and Protestant congregations support themselves is the degree of financial commitment they expect of their members. Most Protestant congregations expect members to make a financial commitment, either through tithing or pledging. Most Catholic parishes rely on voluntary contributions through the collection basket, with no specific financial commitment. My studies show that nearly 40 percent of regular Mass-attending Catholics base their giving on how much is in their checkbook that week. If the checkbook is flush (usually at the beginning of the month), they'll contribute more. If the checkbook is a little low that week, they'll contribute less (or perhaps nothing). If they miss Mass for whatever reason, Catholics frequently don't make up their contributions later. They truly treat their giving as a voluntary act.

It is difficult to imagine a good steward who has not made a commitment. Tithing or pledging are critical components of formalizing that commitment. Making a financial commitment to their parish is often foreign to Catholics, however, who tend to resist. But there are creative ways to make it more attractive. For example, I know of a parish that holds an annual "Commitment Sunday." At Mass on that day, right after the homily, parishioners proceed to the altar and drop their commitment cards (e.g., pledge cards) in a basket. At the end of the procession, the priest starts a fire and dumps the commitment cards in. The message is clear: your commitment is between you and God.

An increasingly popular method of making a financial commitment is through electronic transfers. Parishioners arrange with their bank to have funds automatically transferred from their account to the parish's account, usually at the beginning of the month. This way, they are giving of their "firstfruits," a sound biblical concept. My studies show that when a household starts contributing electronically, its annual contributions increase by 30 percent. Not only do they contribute when their checkbooks are more flush, they contribute whether or not they happen to be at Mass on a particular Sunday.

Some priests object to electronic transfers since they fear it diminishes participation in the offertory. But most offertory envelope companies, like Our Sunday Visitor, now print their envelopes with a check-off box that says, "I have contributed electronically." Thus, parishioners who opt for electronic transfers can still participate in the offertory by dropping these envelopes in the collection basket.

Regardless of how it's done, the practical theology of stewardship requires a financial commitment from parishioners.

8. Stewardship formation and education for all. In order for a parish to become a stewardship parish, it must work at implementing stewardship year-round, as well as age-appropriate stewardship formation for all parishioners. Stewardship should be included in the curriculum for both parochial school religion classes and religious education. There should also be stewardship activities for parish youth groups. Adult education, for its part, should target its stewardship message about the sharing of time, talent, and treasure to its specific audience—whether it's all adults or certain segments, such as widowed, separated and divorced, singles, or married couples—and their status in life.

Because there is such confusion among Catholics about the meaning of stewardship, making it an integral part of parish education and formation activities can help to clear the air.

9. Treat parishioner contributions of time and talent as a ministry, not as a volunteer activity. I have a big problem with the term "parish volunteer." The connotation is that since I'm only a volunteer, it's okay if I show up on time or not because, after all, I'm only a volunteer; or if I do a good job or not in handling my parish duties, after all, I'm only a volunteer.

I much prefer to tell parishioners they're engaged in a ministry, and what they do is vital to the parish. The parish depends on them. In fact, through their baptism they have joined the priesthood of the laity. Parishioners who serve as eucharistic ministers, lectors, ushers, catechists, parish house receptionists, and more are not volunteers. They are ministers carrying out their baptismal vows. And when they view their roles as such, they tend to take them more seriously. It should also be noted that studies have shown as members become more engaged with the parish, they become more generous financial contributors.

But this doesn't happen overnight. Most parishioners start out with a volunteer mentality. It is up to the parish leadership to convert these volunteers into active members of a ministry. To do so, the leadership needs to ensure they are trained, receive support, and, yes, are held accountable. This, of course, requires a certain competence on the part of parish staff. They need to be capable of training and supporting parishioners who are involved in a ministry, and even holding them accountable. The parish is depending on them. And if someone is not performing well in a particular ministry, the parish leadership needs to be informed.

In my parish, we have an annual dinner for those engaged in parish life. We used to call it our "Volunteer Appreciation Dinner." You might not be surprised to learn we've changed the name to our "Ministry Appreciation Dinner."

10. Include stewardship as a key component of the parish pastoral plan. Every parish should be involved in pastoral planning. By including stewardship as a key goal, you underscore its importance and send the message to the entire parish about the need for every ministry to evaluate its role in contributing to the formation of a stewardship parish. The reality is that stewardship won't take off if just a handful of parishioners are promoting it, no matter how dedicated they are. In order for stewardship to be successful, it must permeate every aspect of parish life. Every parish ministry must be involved.

Becoming a Great Parish through Stewardship

As we've seen time and again, good parishes can become great parishes by introducing a stewardship approach. Great not only in the sense of having more resources but in terms of becoming more spiritually driven.

But moving decisively toward stewardship can be a daunting task in a parish where members lack an understanding and appreciation of the concept. It requires considerable education, support, and patience by the parish's leadership and staff. And it requires getting all parishioners on board. It won't happen overnight, and it won't happen if only a handful of parishioners are committed to being a stewardship parish.

While it's important for the pastor to be supportive and actively involved, he shouldn't be the only player, or necessarily the sole leader, of this movement. A special parish stewardship committee should be formed to take the leadership reins. It should be tasked with educating members about the meaning and benefits of stewardship, and with presenting examples of good stewardship already taking place within the parish. As Nouwen proposed, by getting a critical mass of parishioners committed to the notion of stewardship and to its implementation, the pastor can focus on the spiritual aspects and, in the process, markedly strengthen his own vocation.

Endnotes

1. Henri J. M. Nouwen, *A Spirituality of Fundraising*, The Henri Nouwen Spirituality Series (Nashville, TN: Upper Room, 2010).

2. Thomas H. Jeavons and Rebekah Basinger, *Growing Givers' Hearts: Treating Fundraising as Ministry* (San Francisco: Jossey-Bass, 2000). Used by permission.

Communications:
Vitamins or Dessert?

Helen Osman

Sister Mary Ann Walsh, a giant in the world of church communications (she was even mentioned by name in at least one edition of the Associated Press's style guide), had lots of memorable lines about the church and its tenuous approach to communications. Bishops and pastors think about communications as a mother would dessert, she'd say. If there was money left over in the budget, or if there was a special event, we could have dessert or spend money on communications. Otherwise, let's focus on the meat and potatoes of ministry.

She thought that was a terrible way to look at communications. I would agree. Instead of considering communications a nonessential frill, I suggest that parishes (and dioceses) should think of communications as essential an element to the church's ministry as vitamins are to a healthy person's daily diet. Without communications, our parish body becomes weak, susceptible to outside diseases, malnourished. Furthermore, the best way we communicate is when it is so integrated into daily programming and processes that it becomes easily consumed and a delight to receive—just as the best way to get one's vitamins is in well-prepared, natural food that tastes delicious.

So how does a parish go about integrating communications into its daily routine? In the parlance of professionals in the field, it's called a *communications strategy*. An effective communications strategy includes at least three elements: (1) a clear vision, (2) specific audiences, and (3) quality content and channels. Another way of describing this is to use the five Ws of storytelling: *what* and *why* (vision) do you communicate, *how* (content), to *whom* and *when* (audiences). This chapter considers each of those three elements, and then provides some tactical means to implement a communications strategy.

A Clear Vision

A parish recently spent a good deal of money to have a big, lighted marquee placed on its parish property. This beautiful marker provides a way for the parish to communicate what is important to all who drive by on a busy highway. Sometimes it includes a message about an upcoming event. Sometimes there is a greeting such as "Happy Easter!" But always there are the words, "To rent our parish hall, please call 555-1212." The message is definitely loud and clear: we want your money! Oh, and by the way, here's something that might be meaningful to everyone else. Although that parish expended considerable resources to communicate, it may not have taken the time to be strategic about using that marquee. "What" and "why" were they trying to communicate with that signage?

A vision of communications has to begin with the pastor. You have your own *style* of communication. You may be an introvert or an extrovert. You may be a great preacher or prefer to meet with people one-on-one. You don't need to be all things to all people. But you do need to have a vision for what you want people to think about your parish, how they describe the parish, what its reputation is.

Our Catholic Church has been doing "visioning" from its very beginning. Who decided that we would call ourselves Christians and Jesus the Christ? The word "Christ" can be translated as "the Anointed One." From the birth of the church, then, our faith ancestors envisioned themselves as "anointed." Perhaps we shouldn't be surprised that the Roman Empire considered them dangerous.

And over the centuries, the church has used symbols—including words—to indicate what it is and what it means to be a member of this church. Fire, for example, is a symbol of the Holy Spirit. Making the sign of the cross marks us. The words "one," "holy," "catholic," and "apostolic" encapsulate the core values of our organization. Companies have become expert at this practice. They call it trademarking or branding. You need to determine the vision, or the "brand," of your parish—its defining "mark." Is it welcoming? multicultural? impressive? beautiful? serving? spiritual?

Some may want to claim all of those as the parish's vision or brand. While you can certainly make that claim, what happens in reality is either the parish is mediocre in all aspects, or one of these rises to the top in a somewhat organic manner. In other words, the pastor didn't expend enough time and energy to really understand his vision or the lived faith of the parish. Consider your parish's mission statement for clues about what parishioners and the former pastor think its brand should be. Talk with your staff and the parish council. Would they agree with you on the brand, or the defining mark, of the parish?

Once you've settled on your parish's brand or trademark, be sure that your staff, pastoral council, and finance council know it and that all of you are working together to strengthen that brand. If your staff and key leadership don't buy into your concept, if they don't "get" the vision, no one else will either.

Specific Audiences

The second part of a communications strategy is understanding your key communities. Businesses use the phrases "target audiences" or "key stakeholders" to describe this component. I prefer the word "communities" instead of "audiences" since it suggests a back-and-forth type of communications, rather than a one-way street. Dialogue and listening are key attributes of a successful communicator. In his 2014 World Communications Day message, Pope Francis wrote, "The walls which divide us can be broken down only if we are prepared to listen and learn from one another. . . . A culture of encounter demands that we be ready not only to give, but also to receive."[1]

If you are trying to communicate your vision to everyone the same way, you're not going to be successful. You need to know your communities and what makes each one a community. Some examples could be parents of children in the religious education program and the parish school, liturgical ministers, parish and finance councils, lay organizations, daily Mass attendees, or catechists. In some parishes these are all the same people, but in larger parishes they may have different members.

Consider their unique needs and interests. Do any of them feel ostracized or distanced from the parish leadership, or from one another? Are your parish's parents who work multiple jobs, or its single parents, stretched for time? Or do you have a large number of mothers or fathers who stay home with their children? It is necessary for you to understand the potential barriers preventing these communities from receiving your parish's communications. You also need to know what in their lives would resonate with the vision that you have for the parish. For example, if you want your parish to be known as a welcoming parish and you have many single parents, what would help them appreciate that vision? Perhaps providing child care for every event, and communicating that information in a way that encourages parents to utilize the service.

The "when" part of a communications strategy is also about the "who." A good joke is not the only communication that benefits from good timing. Many parishes are learning that emails sent on Saturday mornings are opened more often than emails sent on Friday afternoons. Pulpit announcements made at the end of Mass aren't heard by those who leave after Communion. Putting websites (URL links) in printed bulletins requires extra effort from those who may be only mildly interested in reading about an advocacy effort.

While the pastor has to take ownership of setting the vision—the "what" and the "why" of a communications strategy—you'll most likely find there are parishioners who can take the lead in defining the "who" and the "when." Savvy business owners, marketing or fund-raising professionals, or people with experience in sales typically do this work for a living. Your diocesan communications, development or stewardship staff might also be able to help.

While reaching out to your diocese, also ask if it has any communications policies. Most have published, at the very least, basic communications procedures regarding safe environment policies and issues. As you are building your parish communications strategy and training your staff and volunteers, be sure that everything is consistent with diocesan policies.

To reiterate, it's important that your staff and key parish leadership know your parish's audiences, what their needs are, and the barriers to effectively communicating with them.

Quality Content and Channels

The "how" of a communications strategy tends to get the most attention since it's identified by content and the channels of distribution. In other words, the bulletin, the emails, the website, the signage.

Sometimes this is where a pastor or parish staff want to start when they consider communications. Avoid that temptation. Remember Sr. Mary Ann's analogy? If you aren't providing a healthy vision or considering the needs of your communities, no fancy digital app or shining marquee is going to fix anything.

Content should be well written, with high-quality images and well-crafted visual design. The Gospel message deserves our very best work. One way to ensure that is to set up work flows, or processes, that allow people with the appropriate skills and authority to make the right decisions. The pastor may have the deepest theological training, but he may write the deadliest run-on sentences ever seen. Let a competent English teacher, journalist, or editor form those sentences into something worthy of Hemingway. They can't alter the theological underpinnings, but they can make it easier for your parishioners to understand what you're trying to communicate.

Deadlines should be realistic and logical. And remember, no matter where you are in the sequencing, if someone misses a deadline, there are consequences down the chain. If you just can't get your column to the bulletin editor until Friday morning, don't be surprised if there are errors in it on Sunday morning.

Honor the medium. Marshall McLuhan famously said, "The medium is the message." There's a lot packed into that phrase, including the notion that you have to consider the attributes of the media you intend to use when creating content. For instance, a video longer than two minutes is deadly on the web. A beautiful liturgy becomes tedious and tiring when one experiences it on a tiny screen (unless you happen to be the presider's mother). A blog works well on a website, but you may want to include only a sentence or two and a link if you're going to post it on the parish's Facebook page. There are also practical considerations for specific communication channels, which we'll consider below.

Signage and Directions

Is it clear to the uninitiated? A parish we attended always welcomed newcomers to coffee in the St. Francis room. But in all the years I heard that announcement or read it in the bulletin, I never learned where the St. Francis room was. Consider what is most important to people who are trying to navigate your campus for the first time.

Bulletins

These are among the most time-consuming chores for parish staffs, yet most bulletins don't show it. They tend to be a hodgepodge of events and listings of phone numbers. Fortunate are those parishioners who can actually find some *formation* along with *information* inside their parish's bulletin.

In 2012, a study by the Center for Applied Research in the Apostolate (CARA) found that the parish bulletin was by far the most frequently used channel of communication by Catholics to get information about their parish or the church—even among millennials.[2] If less than half of all Catholics read the bulletin, it's still considerably more than the number who access parish websites. So, try to find ways to tell those bulletin readers about the core mission of your parish. Some pastors publish highlights from their homily or their weekly blog posts in the bulletin. Others use content based on the Sunday Scripture that is available from other sources, including the weekly service myUSCCB from the US Conference of Catholic Bishops. It's also possible to provide short news stories about a service project, include some catechesis in the announcement about the upcoming confirmations, or provide a "teaser" to entice people to go to your website or to read a really interesting article in the diocesan newspaper.

But what about all those event announcements that someone (often the parish secretary) says absolutely must be included? That information must get out to parishioners, but taking up valuable "real estate" inside a parish bulletin may not be the best way to reach people. Consider emailing those announcements to parishioners so that everyone, regardless of whether they attend Sunday Mass, receives the information. In that way the bulletin—replete with more *formation* content—becomes a valid communications channel that enhances the experience of those who have attended Mass.

Email

Marketers tell us that we've come full circle in the world of digital marketing. After trying out advertising on websites, then Facebook, Pinterest, YouTube, and other social media channels, they're discovering that emails are the most effective way to reach people.

Parishes are no different. One pastor told me his staff reports an 80–90 percent open rate on the emails sent to parishioners. "Open rate" tells us how many emails were actually clicked on and "opened" by recipients. Most software programs that provide email management can give you this kind of information. Using email management software also ensures that your emails aren't being blocked by spam filters and that you can monitor "bounce-backs." Some companies that offer website solutions or data management solutions also provide email management. It's worth the investment.

Websites

Many websites have the same feel as parish bulletins: they look like someone opened a box of trinkets and scattered them around. So many shiny jewels, it's hard to decide which one to select. Others require you to click not once, not twice, but maybe three or four times before you find out the Mass schedule or where the parish is located.

A service such as Google Analytics can help you discover *how* people use your website. As a general rule, though, it should serve two purposes:

First, it should be a digital "welcoming kit" for people interested in what your parish provides, such as the sacraments and a sense of community. Typically, the first place people go when searching for anything is the internet. The Barna Group, which does research for churches, nonprofits, and businesses, found in a 2013 study on practicing millennials (18- to 30-year-olds) that 56 percent check out a parish's website before visiting the church.

Be sure your site is built in a way that search engines can find it. If you don't know what that means, find a company that does and pay them to host the site and provide you with a content management system that allows your staff to update content on a regular basis. Don't let your website grow into a monstrosity of pages and broken links. If you want to archive the content, create a separate digital space. And it should be the job of someone other than the pastor to maintain editorial and operational oversight of that content. It could be a parish staff member or an experienced volunteer or team.

Second, consider the website a source of *great* content about the parish. Post photo galleries and short stories or blogs. Then repurpose that content by sharing it on the parish's social media. Again, think about those "seekers" who are looking on the internet for a faith home.

What aspect of your parish's vision would entice them to come to Mass this Sunday?

If your parish is large, or has good funding, consider software that allows integration of email management with a website system. Software that accomplishes this is often known as membership or association management systems. There are even companies that market systems specifically to Catholic parishes, but many parishes use membership management systems that service not only churches but also universities, professional organizations, and fraternal organizations. These systems can also record and accept donations as well as registrations and payments for religious education and other programming.

Social Media

Social media is a source of great angst and consternation for most pastors. Anecdotally, I see less hand-wringing as a younger generation of digitally savvy men move into rectories, but there are still parishes with policies that do not allow staff or priests to post anything about the parish on social media. This is unfortunate since these restrictive parishes are making themselves invisible to a growing number of young Catholics. They are isolating their community from a world that is embracing new technology.

Pope Benedict was the first pope to encourage the church to move into this new world. In fact, he coined a phrase for it: *the digital continent.* In 2009, he wrote, "These technologies are truly a gift to humanity and we must endeavor to ensure that the benefits they offer are put at the service of all human individuals and communities, especially those who are most disadvantaged and vulnerable."[3] To understand the philosophy of the Holy Father and the Holy See regarding the new media, take time to read the World Communications Day messages. These have been issued annually since 1967, but if you are pressed for time, start with the message for 2007.[4] If you feel like a Luddite and are incapable of understanding young people and their odd jargon, these messages provide a strong pastoral rationale for why it's important for your parish to use such channels as Facebook and YouTube. Pope Francis summed up the Vatican's vision well: "The internet, in particular, offers immense possibilities for encounter and solidarity. This is something truly good, a gift from God."[5]

There are good reasons, of course, why parishes are leery of social media. It has a dark side and the medium is not for the uninitiated.

The US Conference of Catholic Bishops provides a set of guidelines that are extremely useful and necessary to read, even if your parish is already using social media. The guidelines provide definitions of terms, best practices, how to administer social media sets, how to use social networks with minors, what to say to staff about personal sites, and how to report and monitor.[6]

Video, Audio, and More

Some parishes maintain a much larger arsenal of communications channels: a televised Mass, for example, or a low-power AM station, or a bookstore. Each of these has attributes that should be leveraged as much as possible, but that's a conversation beyond the scope of this chapter. Suffice it to say that caution is warranted in each case: if the content doesn't serve the vision of the pastor or the needs of the community, there will not be sufficient return on investment.

Media Relations

This is another area pastors often wish would disappear. Indeed, when a reporter calls it's not usually because something marvelous just happened at the parish. The best advice here is to be sure that whoever answers the parish phone knows how to respond to a reporter's call, particularly who to hand it off to. This is an area in which you absolutely want to be sure you're in alignment with diocesan guidelines. Pastors and parish staff can take comfort in the fact the diocesan communications director usually prefers that he or she talk to the reporter, not you.

Crisis communication plans should be integrated into the parish's overall crisis plans. Don't wait for a natural disaster or a human tragedy to strike to begin finding essential phone numbers or figuring out how to send out email blasts. In these events, the secular media—especially radio, television, and social media—can be your best ally in getting the word out quickly.

Sometimes overlooked among the thicket of information outlets today is the diocesan communication channel. Your parishioners may already receive the diocesan newspaper. It's not unreasonable to conclude that its content, or content on the diocesan website and social media that aligns with your parishioners' needs or interests, could supplement your parish's own content and be leveraged to bring people to your parish, either in person or via your communications channels. Theology on Tap, for instance, is a program geared toward young Catholics who may be seeking a parish home. Follow the diocesan social media channels that promote Theology on Tap events and then provide posts that inform young people about your parish's events that might be of interest to them.

As a final thought, the words "communications," "community," and "communion" share a common root. As Pope Francis wrote in the 2014 World Communications Day message, "Good communication helps us to grow closer, to know one another better, and ultimately, to grow in unity."

Our desire for communion should compel us to be not just good communicators, but *Gospel-good* communicators. Our community deserves nothing less.

Endnotes

1. Message of Pope Francis for the 48th World Communications Day, Communication at the Service of an Authentic Culture of Encounter, June 1, 2014, https://w2.vatican.va/content/francesco/en/messages/communications /documents/papa-francesco_20140124_messaggio-comunicazioni-sociali.html.

2. Mark Gray and Mary Gautier, *Catholic New Media Use in the United States, 2012*, CARA, http://www.usccb.org/about/communications/upload /Catholic_New_Media_Use_in_United_States_2012.pdf.

3. Message of Holy Father Benedict XVI for the 43rd World Communications Day, New Technologies, New Relationships: Promoting a Culture of Respect, Dialogue and Friendship, May 24, 2009, http://w2.vatican.va /content/benedict-xvi/en/messages/communications/documents/hf_ben-xvi _mes_20090124_43rd-world-communications-day.html.

4. Message of Benedict XVI for 41st World Communications Day, Children and the Media: A Challenge for Education, May 20, 2007, http://w2.vatican .va/content/benedict-xvi/en/messages/communications/documents/hf _ben-xvi_mes_20070124_41st-world-communications-day.html.

5. Message of Francis for 48th World Communications Day, Communication at the Service of an Authentic Culture of Encounter.

6. USCCB, Social Media Guidelines, http://www.usccb.org/about/commu nications/social-media-guidelines.cfm.

10

Tools for Leadership Development

Michael Brough

In over twenty years of working with and training priests in a dozen different countries around the world, what's impressed me the most is how all of you want to be the best priest, the best pastor, the best leader possible for the people you serve. At the Leadership Roundtable, we've learned a great deal about how to develop leaders—lay and ordained—in the Catholic Church. And my goal is to impart to you some of those insights to help better prepare you for your challenging role as pastor.

Let's start with a brief introduction to the leadership role of a pastor. You are a leader, but who do you lead? What do you lead? What formation have you received in preparation for that leadership role? To help answer those questions, we're going to look at three different aspects of leadership for the ministry and the essential tools for developing those competencies. We're going to focus on leading yourself, leading others, and leading the organization. Those, in sum, are what parish leadership is about.

For all of us as Catholic leaders, a model of perfect servant leadership exists in John 13:1-15, where Jesus washes the feet of his disciples. In our own ministry, we are called to grow in the likeness of Jesus so that we can more accurately reflect his life and communicate his message. We understand we can only appreciate and truly understand the meaning of that leadership and ministry as we exercise it, and as we reflect upon both our words and our actions. We had a great reminder from our Holy Father Pope Francis as he began his Petrine ministry, counseling us that "authentic power is service."

It's important for us to always look at our pastoral leadership in terms of a spirituality of leadership. I have a favorite quotation from Jean Vanier, that wonderful leader of the L'Arche communities, who said, "Leaders of communities need to *organize* the community so that each member is in the right place and things work smoothly. They need to *animate* it, so that it continues to be alive and the eyes of all are fixed on the essential goals. They need to *love* each person and be concerned about their growth."[1]

So organize, animate, and love: three elements of our pastoral leadership ministry. Priests have told us over the years that some of those leadership skills have been taught to them better than others. Some they've learned in the seminary, some from experienced priests and lay leaders, and some through ministry situations in the parish. The four tools offered in this chapter are designed specifically to help develop those leadership skills required of you as pastor of a parish. To reinforce them, I'm going to share with you some lessons we've learned at the Leadership Roundtable through a project we developed called Catholic Leadership 360 (www.CatholicLeadership360.org). It's a unique collaboration with the National Federation of Priests' Councils and the National Association of Church Personnel Administrators to develop leaders, both lay and ordained, within the church. We also benefited from the research and educational products of the Center for Creative Leadership (www.CCL.org), which informs the four tools offered in this chapter.

Assessing the Need for Leadership Development

We'll begin our discussion of leadership development with a number of questions that I'm sure have arisen within your own ministry. How do you know how well you're doing as a leader? How can new pastors learn how to become good pastors? How can you tell your leadership strengths and development needs? And how do we encourage accountability for the ongoing formation of priests?

Fortunately, the US Conference of Catholic Bishops addressed these issues in their 1984 document on the need for the continuing formation of priests. They described it as "a lifelong dialogue journey through which a priest comes to greater awareness of one's self, others, and God. Personal growth, continuing formation, theological education, and human development. All of which lead to greater service of the people of God. These are woven throughout the priest's entire life and ministry."

The bishops were even more explicit in their 2005 document *Co-Workers in the Vineyard of the Lord*. Here, they speak of the need for evaluation and feedback for those of us in ministry, for formal written appraisals within the context of our mission (in this case as pastor), and for recognizing that we have both deficiencies we need to work on and strengths that need to be recognized and developed or leveraged. *Co-Workers* states,

> In a comprehensive personnel system, this area [evaluation and feedback] addresses regular performance appraisals, as a part of ministerial workplace practice, that provide a formal opportunity for every individual minister to reflect on his or her own performance and get feedback from a supervisor and that may include the views of colleagues and those served. Appraisal and feedback is most effective when conducted in the context of the mission of the parish or diocese. Documentation of honest and constructive feedback about deficiencies and subsequent steps for improvement is important, as is both formal and informal recognition of generous, Christ-centered, and effective service.[2]

With that as backdrop, here are some specific lessons we've learned working with priests:

First, we need leadership development that creates adaptive solutions. We don't learn how to be leaders for a fixed situation. We're faced with changing conditions, unexpected happenings, and new people coming into the situation.

Second, we need leadership development that expands the leadership space. That means involving others in leadership. It means using and developing persuasive skills for working with others. It means being respectful, building trust between those we lead and ourselves.

Third, we need to develop reflective leaders. Priests are particularly good at this. It's part of the formation that we go through as Catholic ministry leaders—where solutions emerge from prayer, discernment, and dialogue. Solutions emerge over time with reflection.

Fourth, we need help on how to identify priorities. This is perhaps the biggest challenge many pastors face. How do we identify our priorities? How do we manage our time? How do we make sure that we are accessible to people? How do we use our time in both formal and informal settings within the parish?

And finally, we need leadership development that is responsible to the church, that reflects the values and beliefs of the church, and that is open to a broader understanding of who we are as the church and what it means to be *church*.

Perhaps the most important lesson we've learned is that for development to really work it requires three different components: assessment, challenge, and support. If you put those three elements together, then you have a better chance of growth. But in our work with pastors and priests we've come to realize that for leadership development to really work well it must be within the broader context of diocese and ministry. In other words, I recognize that my leadership development is not simply something I do alone, but that other priests are going through that same development at the same time as part of a broader, shared mission, and that there are ways for us to connect and to support one another in that process.

Having said that, let's take a look at four essential leadership development tools pastors should have in their toolbox.

Tool One: Identify Competencies

What do I mean by leadership competencies? Our partners at the Center for Creative Leadership describe competencies as measurable characteristics of a person that are related to success at work. A competency may be a behavioral skill such as acting fairly, not playing favorites. It could be a technical skill such as public speaking. It could be an attribute such as intelligence or it could be an attitude such as optimism.

There are literally hundreds of leadership competencies. What we've done at the Leadership Roundtable, and in the Catholic Leadership 360 program, is select thirteen pastoral leadership competencies from three different sources: *Pastores Dabo Vobis* (1992), the *Basic Plan for the Ongoing Formation of Priests* (2001), and *In Fulfillment of Their Mission* (2008), a document on the duty and tasks of Roman Catholic priests. These cover a broad range of competencies required of a priest, such as communicating ideas and information, inspiring commitment from others, bringing out the best in people, forging synergy, developing relationships, having respect for differences between individuals and groups, and selecting and developing people to work within ministry. They also include competencies like courage, openness, and flexibility, and a willingness to learn and a commitment to personal ongoing formation. These competencies are combined with specific ministerial competencies that relate to your identity and your role as pastor and priest. In other words, how can you be most effective in your priestly ministry?

Let's take a closer look at one of those competencies: How effective are you in communicating ideas and information? And to that end, what are the specific behaviors and skills you require as pastor? Some are written communication skills, while others are verbal capabilities that help determine how well you impart ideas and vision in a parish council meeting, for example. Another example of a competency is being able to overcome resistance that sometimes occurs when you're trying to communicate a particular message.

Tool Two: Gather Feedback

As leadership guru Ann Morrison reminds us in *Breaking the Glass Ceiling*, "While perceptions may not be the ultimate truth, they are what people use to make decisions."[3] So, gathering feedback is important. Understanding how you are perceived as a leader is important. Of course, you get feedback informally from people all the time in the parish. But how can you get formal feedback that will help you to develop leadership competencies—the leadership skills—that you require as pastor? Let's consider four relevant questions:

First, who should you ask for feedback from? The best sort of feedback is 360-degree feedback. As the name suggests, that means not just from one person, like your boss or someone you work with or a direct-report or someone you serve, but rather from *all* of these. Ask for feedback from people who know you and the role you're being asked to play, and who are willing to give an honest answer so that you can learn and grow from it. Identify as many people as possible who may be in a position to offer you their perceptions. The more feedback you receive, the more you can remove layers of subjectivity and arrive at bigger-picture conclusions.

Second, when is a good time to ask for feedback? The answer, of course, is constantly so that you can get feedback on a regular basis and see the results of adjustments you're making. But it's very important to ask for feedback when there is a specific competency or leadership development skill that you're looking to focus on and improve. If I've received feedback that says, "Michael, you really could work on your communication skills," then it's good for me to ask people, "Okay, let's talk about which communication skills I need to improve, and can you give me feedback on them?"

Third, how should you ask for feedback? In addition to the generalities that informal feedback tends to produce, it's important to collect some formal feedback. That means asking people directly, "Can you describe for me the specific *situation* in which you've observed this behavior?" "What specific *behaviors* did you observe?" "And can you tell me the *impact* that behavior had?" That allows you to know as a person trying to develop your leadership skills what you need to focus on. It's important to note that we're not talking here about personality-driven leadership. Some people like our style, others don't. Some people like our personality, others don't. That's not what we're talking about developing here. We're talking instead about getting feedback on specific behaviors—because we can change behaviors. Personality, we're stuck with!

Fourth, how should you use the feedback you receive? Focus on the future, not the past. The feedback will by definition refer to past events, but how can you use the information to change future encounters? Some of the best advice here is to focus on one particular competency you've received feedback on and ask yourself, "How am I going to improve in this area?" If you're dedicated to making a change and acknowledging that this is the behavior you want to work on, then you can make a difference. The other way to use feedback is to evaluate it carefully, since not all feedback is equal. Which leads us to the question, How do you interpret feedback? Well, you know what it's like at the end of Sunday Mass when everyone walks past and you shake hands. "Great sermon, Father," someone says, but the next ten walk past and don't reference the sermon at all. So is that helpful feedback? Is it just one person who thought it was a great sermon, or is it that the others didn't take the time to tell you? Or did the others think it was merely average, or maybe terrible and they're not coming back? So informal feedback is fine, but it's not nearly as helpful as getting ongoing formal feedback from people. One small piece of feedback is not the whole picture. It's a snapshot. It gives you a useful piece of information, but then you need to interpret the data.

I've seen two common mistakes in terms of how people interpret feedback. The first is that they agree too quickly. "Oh yes, that's me all right; not much I can do about it." The second is that they disagree too quickly. "That's not true. That's not who I am." Both reactions are counterproductive. It's important to take time to reflect upon the feedback you've received—particularly if it's focused feedback—and decide how you're going to respond.

Tool Three: Create a Development Plan

Don't panic. This isn't as complicated as it might sound, especially if you follow these four steps:

First, identify your strengths and development needs. You can understand these in four different ways. One way is your confirmed strengths, where you receive feedback that says, "Okay, you're really good at this." You always thought you were, so this is now a confirmed strength. Then there are unrecognized strengths, areas you didn't know you were good at but where people said through their feedback, "Yes, this is how you come across. This is how we experience your leadership." The third way is confirmed development needs: somebody gives you feedback that suggests "you need to work on this," and you acknowledge, "Yes, this is an area I know from past experience I need to work on." And fourth is unrecognized development needs. These are the blind spots—areas you didn't realize you needed help with until feedback alerted you to your shortcomings.

Second, create a development plan to prioritize the feedback you receive. In other words, how important is this feedback for your ministry? Yes, you'd like to develop this or that skill, but is it really important to you at this time? Looking ahead, what challenges will you face in your pastoral leadership over the next year or two? Obviously, if you can develop a skill you know you're going to need, that will allow you to meet those challenges more effectively. And two final questions in terms of prioritizing feedback: Is it worth the time and effort it will take to make changes in this area, and how motivated are you to undertake those changes? Frankly, this requires you to be very honest with yourself because if you don't have the motivation—even if it's an area that needs development—it's probably best to choose another area where you're more likely to be successful. As a rule of thumb, as long as your weaknesses are not derailments (i.e., as long as they do not stop you from being effective in your ministry), it is more worthwhile to further develop your strengths.

Third, identify and articulate your goals. Let's be clear here—we're not talking about a five-page document listing a whole bunch of goals. I'm suggesting instead that two or three development goals at any one time are sufficient. My experience in working with and coaching others is that if you identify one goal to focus on and prove to be successful with it, then you're more likely to come back to goals two and three and try to develop them. Don't overreach. Choosing goals that are important to you and that you can commit to accomplishing is the best formula for success. As with any goals, of course, they should be clear, specific, and assessable. And there should be a time frame for completing them, along with specific action steps: "This is what I'm going to do. These are the behaviors I'm going to change." And finally, be clear about the outcomes. In other words, "I expect within the time frame I've set to be able to accomplish this or that." If you don't set clear outcomes, you'll never know if you've achieved your goals.

Fourth, and finally, make sure you follow through. This, unfortunately, is often neglected, leading to tremendous frustration. It's pointless to go through the process of getting feedback, identifying competencies to improve, and creating goals if you don't intend to follow through. This means not just responding to feedback you've already received but responding to feedback you *continue* to receive. Holding yourself accountable is the key here. Best practice calls for sharing your development goals with others to help you hold yourself accountable, as well as to solicit their help and support. Set a specific time to review whether or not you've achieved your goals. This may involve meeting with a supervisor, superior, coach, or friend—someone who will hold you accountable. In the end, this is a very adult model for learning and for ensuring leadership development.

To help firm up for you what I mean by setting concrete goals, here's an example I've adapted from feedback specialists Karen Kirkland and Sam Manoogian in their practical guidebook, *Ongoing Feedback*:[4]

> I will improve my effectiveness in leading my pastoral team by concentrating on the following two goals. I will learn to reserve judgment on others' ideas by making sure that my initial response is not a negative one. Additionally, I will ask for input from the group before

decisions are made or finalized. I will ask Deacon Jose, a friend and mentor, to give me feedback and help me monitor my progress. I will achieve these goals by July 1st, six months from now.

You can see in these goals the infrastructure of a sound development plan:

- Here's the behavior I'm going to change.
- Here are the specific goals to make that happen.
- Here's how I plan to get feedback and monitor my progress.
- Here's the timeline I've set.

Tool Four: Engage Support/Identify a Coach

You are more likely to be successful developing your leadership skills if you create developmental relationships. These relationships fulfill three essential functions: *assessment*—helping you assess your performance on a continuing basis; *challenge*—pushing you beyond your normal comfort zone; *support*—providing both ministry and personal support.

One of the most effective forms of support in working with priests and bishops—something that's observable in the secular realm as well—is a coach. Coaching is defined as helping, motivating, enabling people—professionally and/or personally—to determine a direction and move swiftly toward their goals. Indeed, it's about helping people transition from where they are to where they want to be. A coach can be invaluable in helping you grow your competence, commitment, and confidence. He or she can make the difference between a leadership development plan that succeeds and one that fails.[5]

Reflecting on the Journey Ahead

In concluding this chapter on leadership development, here are some questions to reflect on:

- What have you learned about leading yourself?
- What have you learned about leading others?

- What have you learned about leading your organization?
- What leadership competency can you commit yourself to work on and improve?
- What further assistance do you need in order to be able to develop these skills?

As you focus on the commitment you've made to your ongoing formation and development, you have my hopes and prayers, as well as those of your parishioners, that you may continue to develop the requisite skills and become leaders as fathers, as brothers, and as companions on the journey of faith. As our Holy Father Pope Francis put it, speaking to male religious in November 2013,

> In life it is difficult for everything to be clear, precise, outlined neatly. . . . Life is complicated; it consists of grace and sin. . . . We all make mistakes and we need to recognize our weaknesses. . . . We always must think of the people of God in all of this. Just think of religious who have hearts that are as sour as vinegar: they are not made for the people. In the end we must not form administrators, managers, but fathers, brothers, traveling companions.[6]

Endnote

1. Jean Vanier, *Community and Growth*, rev. ed. (Mahwah, NJ: Paulist Press, 1989), 208.

2. US Bishops, *Co-Workers in the Vineyard of the Lord: A Resource for Guiding the Development of Lay Ecclesial Ministry* (Washington, DC: USCCB, 2005), .

3. Ann Morrison and others, *Breaking the Glass Ceiling: Can Women Reach the Top of America's Largest Corporations?*, updated ed. (New York: Perseus, 1992), 24.

4. Karen Kirkland and Sam Manoogian, *Ongoing Feedback: How to Get It, How to Use It* (Greensboro, NC: Center for Creative Leadership, 2004).

5. For further resources to help you achieve your development goals, visit www.CatholicLeadership360.org.

6. Joshua McElwee, "Pope Calls Religious to Be 'Real Witnesses,'" *National Catholic Reporter* (January 14, 2014).

Taking Charge of Your Time
and Focusing Your Energy

Jim Dubik

We have all the time there is. So the real question is whether we use all the time we have well or poorly. But even that question doesn't quite get to the heart of the matter. When you come right down to it, time is a metaphor for energy and focus. When we ask ourselves whether we're using our time well, the question we're really asking—or should be asking—is this: Am I focusing my energy on the important or trivial? Time is just the way we measure where we place our focus and energy. In this chapter I hope to present a way to first think through what is important relative to your role as pastor and then translate the result of that thinking into a way to increase the probability of focusing on the important. No methodology is perfect; we shouldn't expect that, especially those of us who lead people in human organizations—that is, all of us. But a disciplined approach to managing time should increase the time you spend on the important.

I've been lucky in my life. I've had over thirty-seven years of experience as an army officer leading mission-driven organizations, some as small as twenty and others as large as forty-six thousand; some were all-American organizations and others were made up of multiple nationalities and religions; sometimes my unit was located in one geographic place and other times it was dispersed over dozens of locations; sometimes I led in war and other times at peace. But, I've not had a job. My life has been a life of service to something larger than myself, and I've led people who wanted to connect their lives to something greater than self. As I reflect on that life, I was never overbusy when I was involved in something important. Rather, I was excited and so were those I led, for our lives had meaning. I imagine it's been the same for you!

Throughout much of my career, I've employed the time-management program that I advocate in this chapter. I didn't need a "system" when I was leading small organizations, but that didn't last long. As soon as I started working on a staff of a large organization, I realized that I needed a way to make sure I was focused on the right stuff. And when I started to command, even as a deputy commander, that need smacked me in the face. Some of the approach I will describe I learned in the school of hard knocks. But some I learned through the advice and example of seniors, peers, and juniors as well as through reading and experimenting.[1]

The processes that I use in this chapter are drawn from my military experience. Each of you reading will have to evaluate what I suggest to determine how to adapt the methodology to fit your particular situation as pastors, just as I had to adapt what worked in the corporate world to fit my military world. My intuition is that much of what I write will be useful to you, but some of it may not be. None of us can simply take what works in one context and apply it blindly to another. But we can learn from one another and modify best practices from one context to fit another.

Before I begin, however, I think a few words about leadership and management are in order. From my perspective the two are related, but different. You lead people and manage things. Leadership is about relating people to each other and to a common purpose. Leadership is essentially a "ministry of presence." You have to know and be with people to lead them. You have to share in their lives, participate in their celebrations and sorrows. Paratroopers have a saying: It's hard to be uppity when you're jumping from the same plane, hitting the same ground, and living in the same hole. Leaders create followers by their presence and their example. Leaders create followers by providing vision, direction, and motivation. "Follow me" is the motto of the US infantry, not "Go that way; I'll be with you in a minute."

Management is about efficiency. You manage things, processes, and resources. Management is about organizing ways of doing things into transparent, repeatable processes so that the organization runs smoothly. Management affects mission as much as leadership. Soldiers don't follow commanders, even if they're great leaders, whose units run poorly. For example, when transportation doesn't arrive on time, mail is always late, promotions arrive but the corresponding pay does not, equipment doesn't work because maintenance isn't done on schedule, or food and resupply show up late or go to the wrong place altogether—soldiers don't conclude that they have a great leader; they conclude that they're in a screwed-up unit. Furthermore, they realize that they can't accomplish their mission under this kind of poor management. Followers are pretty savvy people. They link three things together, correctly so in my view: mission, leadership, and management.

So creating a time-management approach is a matter of freeing up time to lead, preserving and regenerating the energy to lead, and ensuring the management of the organization is efficient. Now, we're ready to start.

Thinking

We have only one life, and it's a multidimensional life. Simultaneously we could be a son or a daughter, a brother or a sister, an aunt or an uncle, and a leader and a follower. Each of our lives has a spiritual dimension as well as physical, intellectual, and moral dimensions. We each live in a complex set of contexts: family, social, political, and religious—to name just a few. Figuring out what's important, therefore, is a lot harder than it seems on the surface; each of us has to answer some hard questions. And even after we answer them, things will change. That's because life never stands still. You can't put your life on pause, so to speak, while you're leading an organization. So any methodological approach to managing time has to fit the reality in which we live and lead.

Step One: Identify Your Big Rocks

The first challenge you face is how to "fill the jar" of your life. In his *First Things First*, Stephen Covey asks us to imagine the challenge of getting big rocks, little rocks, and sand into a container.[2] If you fill the jar with sand and the little rocks first, you won't get the big rocks in. The question is: What are your big rocks? Big rocks come in two categories: personal and organizational.

Your personal big rocks first have to do with what you need to preserve and regenerate leadership energy, and second, with maintaining key relationships in your life. I knew, for example, that when I deployed to Baghdad in 2007 and 2008, leadership in that environment would take a heavy emotional toll, and every day I would have to start afresh. To do that, I'd have to be at my best, which meant that I'd have to get proper rest (and for me that's six to eight hours a night), have a vigorous workout schedule (one to two hours a day), time for prayer (one hour a day), and time for writing letters necessary to maintain my relationship with my wife, children, brothers and sisters, dad, and friends (another hour a day). The total time for personal big rocks came to ten to twelve hours a day. I reduced this by one hour by using as prayer time the time in flight or transit from Baghdad to one of the many activities for which my unit was responsible. That left thirteen to fifteen hours a day for "work." That time was filled with my organizational big rocks.

Step Two: Discover Your Organizational Big Rocks and Perennials

You're going to need some help with discovering "organizational big rocks" and what might be called "perennials." Organizational big rocks come in two varieties: leading and managing.

To discover your leadership big rocks, you'll have to analyze your parish and ask some questions. You start with getting an understanding of where your parish is—what it does well and what it does not so well, what part of its mission is strong and what part might be weak, where your parish is healthy and where it is sick, and where in the parish your people are thriving and where they may be floundering. Starting here will help you identify where your parish is and where it ought to go. Leadership takes place in the space between "is" and "ought."

Once you know where your parish is strongest, you'll have to allocate enough time to maintain that strength. Don't assume maintaining strength can be put on autopilot. You will not have to allocate a lot of time to maintenance, but you'll have to allocate some. You'll want to visit these activities enough to keep them going strong. So list these strengths and figure out how often you have to visit them to keep them on track (daily? weekly? monthly? quarterly? semiannually?). You can figure this out by talking to both the leaders and participants of each activity.

Then analyze your parish's areas of weakness. This may take a bit of time too. To get an adequate understanding of what is really wrong, you will probably have to have a set of discussions with leaders in the various parts of your parish as well as those who may work with them. Once you have a good sense, you will then be able to determine how often you have to visit with them to do your part in improving whatever is awry. Once things seem back on track, then you'll be able to reassess your frequency allocation.

You will have some "management big rocks" too. Every organization has them. Personnel, finance, facilities and equipment maintenance, training, ministry planning, supplies, and logistics—all are examples. You should try to make a complete list of the management expectations that your parish has of you. As with your "leadership big rocks," you will have to map these out with regard to frequency. Which of these management responsibilities are weekly, monthly, quarterly, semiannually, or annually? In some cases, you will find that they are ad hoc—that is, they don't happen on a routine schedule. (Note: You should change "ad hoc" to "preplanned." Your parish will run more smoothly.)

Finally, identify your recurring responsibilities—your "perennials." Every leadership position has these. Some will be representative. For example, in one of my commands, every February I had to hand out awards at the annual volunteer recognition dinner, every March I had to represent the Armed Services in a local city's parade, every July I was expected to open the Fourth of July celebration, and every December I participated in a tree-lighting ceremony. Others will be meetings or conferences that your bishop may expect you to attend—monthly, quarterly, semiannually, or annually. Still others might be reports that only you can write.

If you're lucky, you can look at your predecessor's calendar and find these events. If you're not so lucky, then you may have to ask someone to help you do the investigative work to create this list. Lucky or not, identifying these kinds of responsibilities early prevents surprises later on.

Without doubt, once you've discovered your big rocks and perennials, you will be like I have been many times—realizing that I can't possibly meet all these demands. Be not afraid, you have reached the assessing and divesting phase of step two.

Put all your big rocks and perennials on a calendar, or do a matrix, or whatever display with which you are comfortable. A visual is important at this phase because now you will have to determine which, among the many things you seem to have to do—or that others are expecting you to do—are those that you really must do. On your visual, mark those you must do and those that only you can do. The rest are opportunities to divest—in the words of a former boss of mine, "Opportunities to allow others to shine."

Do this analysis with the help of a set of trusted leaders in your parish. I would often do this assessment with my deputy, my senior enlisted adviser, and my subordinate commanders—five to eight people. I have always found wisdom emerged from such collaboration. When a group saw the full nature of the challenge, each member felt a need to help identify solutions. In a parish, especially one where a pastor may not even have an assistant, the group should include one or two members of the staff and another two or three lay leaders.

You will want to set up a "we're in this together" dynamic in the group looking at your visual. If you are able to do that, members will start thinking out loud. You want to get to the point in the discussion where they begin to suggest that some of what you have identified as things only you can do are things one of them can actually do. And you want to get the discussion to the point where members look at the things you have on the visual but not identified as "your tasks" and say either "that's not a reasonable expectation, let's do that another way," or "you can't possibly do that, let's ask so-and-so to take that on." In this way, you can begin divesting those responsibilities and expectations to others in the parish.

Doing so frees time for you to lead and focus only on the important management tasks. Divesting also develops leadership capacity throughout your parish and creates cohesion among your parish leadership team. Divesting always surprised me. In these discussions, some people who stepped up to take on a task were those I didn't expect would—either because they were, mistakenly in my mind, too inexperienced, unwilling, or already too busy. If no one steps up, either you've identified something that your parish really doesn't have to do, or you've found a necessary activity in need of a leader. Finally, once you've finished divesting, set up a monthly meeting for those who have accepted new responsibilities so that they have a forum to keep you informed of their actions and in which they can ask for more guidance if they need it.

We're now ready for the last step in the thinking phase.

Step Three: Allocate Percentages, Get a Sanity Check, and Adjust

Now it's time to ask yourself, how much energy must I spend on leading and managing? The answer to this question will come in a time percentage.

Remember, the time you need to regenerate comes "off the top." By way of example, let's use eleven hours as regeneration time and thirteen hours as leadership and management time. This means that 46 percent of each day is allocated to regenerating your leadership energy. It also means that 54 percent of the time, you will be fully energized for your parish—that's 54 percent that will go toward the leadership tasks that you've identified and to your management tasks and perennials, as well.

You should end up with a leadership and management task list and an appropriate time allocation, one that fits the needs of your parish as you and your team determine it.

Executing

In most organizations, the secretary or administrative assistant has the responsibility to prepare the leader's schedule. In some larger organizations, that responsibility may be shared among a chief of staff, a personal assistant, and an executive assistant. In some smaller organizations, like a parish, the pastoral leader may do his own schedule. In what follows, I address those situations where the pastor is doing his own schedule.

Set Some Boundaries and Rules

Creating your schedule needs some ground rules. Here are some examples:

- All meetings have an agenda, a person in charge, and start and end times.
- Meetings will run no more than two hours, unless approved beforehand.
- Travel time between meeting and events is part of the schedule.
- Allocate at least fifteen minutes between meetings, if no travel time is involved.
- Start the daily schedule at 9:00 a.m. (unless you've got an earlier Mass), and don't schedule anything after 6:00 p.m., unless it's an approved official function (like a parish council meeting).
- Schedule no more than three evening functions per week.

- Schedule no official public functions on your day off.
- Stop the official schedule at 3:30 p.m. the day before your day off.

Your rules will be different. They will reflect your personality and style as well as the needs of your parish and the demands your mission places upon you.

I also limited advance distribution of my calendars. Only key members of my staff had access before the schedules were locked in. Early in my leadership development, I opened access to all. That was a mistake. What I found was that subordinate leaders, staff, and even community leaders would look for "white space" (that is, time on the schedule with nothing on it) and attempt to fill it up. As a leader, I wanted to preserve "white space" for thinking or spontaneity—or prayer! Ultimately, I learned how to limit access so that the right set of people could collaborate in creating my schedule and calendar but not so many that the scheduling lost its discipline.

Rules like these create boundaries for your parish staff. Without them, a pastor's life can easily become a solely professional or public affair. Or life can become so harried that it is unlivable. Rules like these are also necessary to preserve a pastor's regenerative time. And they're necessary as a "prioritization-forcing function." A leader normally has more to do than time to do it. Putting boundaries in place forces you (and your parish staff) to prioritize and divest constantly. Of course, there are exceptions to every rule at times, but that's what they are, exceptions, not the rule.

Create a Schedule, Follow It, and Note Changes

With the rules and time allocations in place and your big rocks and perennials identified, you can get to work on creating your schedule, and then following it. This step may seem self-evident, but it is not. Following the schedule is important for several reasons. It demonstrates a level of organizational integrity—that is, the organization and the leaders within it do what they say they're going to do. Following the schedule also produces predictability within your parish and creates the space for your staff to use their initiative. When a staff member knows that he or she will see the pastor on a predictable schedule, that staff member is less tempted to conduct a "hallway ambush" or have a "drive-by" office call.

Predictability helps you, as well. You'll know that the "big rocks and perennials" methodology ensures a visit to every key aspect of the parish organization and every staff member at a prescribed frequency. Emergencies always happen, and every leader should stay open to them. But, absent emergencies, following a schedule based on a well-thought-out methodology can be a stabilizing force within your parish.

At the end of the day, review how the actual day compared to the schedule. Doing so will provide the grist for the next aspect of the time-management methodology: assessing and adapting.

One final word: When creating your own schedule, as I do now in retirement, the actions above are still necessary. In fact, they may be more necessary because acting alone provides less oversight and increases the chances of poor use of a leader's time.

Assessing and Adapting

Once a month, a good pastoral leader should review how he actually spent time relative to the time-allocation goals set. The purpose is not just a factual review but an opportunity to analyze why execution differed from goals and then to adjust goals, if necessary. The review should also include a task/frequency matrix. The matrix provides the leader another view as to whether he or she is focused on the important.

If the difference between actual and planned time is small, you can usually ignore the difference. But in those cases where the difference is large, the pastor must dive deeper to understand why the difference emerged. Further, month-to-month differences also require investigation. Sometimes, the differences are explained by an unusual set of circumstances or requirements. So no adjustments are needed. Other times, the disparity lacks an adequate explanation, so reinforcing methodological discipline may be in order. When a disparity persists, however, the pastor must question the allocation of time, figure out a way to divest some of the tasks in that category, or identify other corrective actions. But all these decisions are data-based; further, the data results from the goals set because of a thorough leadership and management analysis.

Absent a time-management system like the one described, a leader usually has no idea how he or she is spending time or focusing energy— the pastoral leader's most important resources.

Conclusion

At first blush you may think that using a system like this is too much. I ask you to think again. Most of the work necessary to use this kind of methodology is "up-front" leadership work: the kind of organizational analysis any good leader does when he or she comes to a new organization, or the kind good leaders do periodically to ensure their organization is doing what it should be doing and operating as efficiently as possible. Further, it's the kind of analysis that a good leader does to ensure the organization's mission and its staff are fully supported and free of obstacles the organization itself creates to inhibit accomplishing its mission.

I've seen some really creative uses of a leader's time. Some, for example, use meals as "leadership time." One commander held weekly breakfasts at his house, rotating different groups of leaders each week; another used weekly lunches at various dining facilities throughout his command for the same reasons but with different sets of leaders. I've also seen some leaders use their exercise time to invite selected members of their command, some leaders and others not, to run with them. One way to look at "tricks" like these is from the perspective of maximizing the use of time. Another way is from the perspective of preserving regenerative time.

However leaders approach their time, time management remains a surrogate for the ways in which leaders focus their energy and attention on the important. We have all the time there is, and if leaders use it well, most often it's enough. I guess it *has* to be because we're not getting any more.

Endnotes

1. Three of the books I use on a recurring basis are these: Stephen R. Covey, A. Roger Merrill, and Rebecca R. Merrill, *First Things First* (New York: Free Press, 1994); Jim Loehr and Tony Schwartz, *The Power of Full Engagement* (New York: Free Press, 2003); and Stephen Rechtschaffen, *Time Shifting: Creating More Time to Enjoy Your Life* (New York: Doubleday, 1996).

2. See Covey, Merrill, and Merrill, *First Things First*, 88ff.

12

A Pastor's Wellness

Andrew F. Kelly

At a convention on training for the priesthood, Pope Francis observed that young men who are psychologically unstable without knowing it often seek strong structures to support them, such as the police or the army, but for some it is the clergy: "When I realize that a young man is too rigid, too fundamentalist, I do not have confidence [about him]; in the background there is something that he himself does not know. . . . [Keep your] eyes open to the mission in seminaries."[1]

For the past twenty-five years, as director of the Clergy Consultation and Treatment Service at St. Vincent's Hospital in Westchester, New York, I've had the honor of working with hundreds of priests who have welcomed me into their interior lives. My goal in this chapter is to share with you some of that knowledge and experience in the hope you may avoid in your priesthood the kind of problems I've observed in others. It's also my fervent hope you will learn the skills of awareness, healthy coping, and self-care that can lead to a happy and fulfilling life as a pastor.

Because the priesthood is more a way of life than just a job, it's useful to our discussion to pose this question at the outset: *Whose priesthood is it?* You need to be clear on this. You're not doing it for mom, dad, or someone else. You're not doing it for the external reward of prestige, or because you need a ready-made role/identity. And you're not doing it to work out internal conflicts, which are best solved through the adoption of a code of conduct.

We start with this question because you cannot build a solid internal structure on external needs. To be sure, your priesthood will collapse without a strong internal foundation. For that reason, there can be only one answer to the question, Whose priesthood is it? *It has to be yours.*

Separating from the Laity

One approach to the theory of role identity sees a strong distinction between priests and laypeople. It holds that some people enter the priesthood to adopt a ready-made identity, to overcome a core of shame, and may use ordination as a way to bolster self-esteem and set themselves apart from others. In this version, negative qualities that could be associated with the laity (lust, substance abuse, depression, neediness, and being victimized as a child) are minimized by adoption of the in-group identity of clergy. The danger here is a failure to recognize the real self, as in "I am not one of them—I am a priest." Equally troublesome is its corollary, "I do not really need to be concerned with *me*. That is selfish. I care for others."

What this disconnection ignores is the fact you are a human being entrusted with the care of yourself. You have the same human needs, the same temptations and risks as the laity. To attempt to compensate for this by adopting an identity is not dealing with one's issues—it's to bury, camouflage, and deny them. It's to deny internal awareness. Also implicit in this approach is an effort to diminish the laity and elevate oneself, which runs counter to what the church teaches in the *Program for Priestly Formation*. It holds, "A man of communion [is] a person who has real and deep relational capacities, someone who can enter into genuine dialogue and friendship, a person of true empathy who can understand and know other persons."[2] How does one accomplish this by setting oneself apart?

Caring for yourself is essential. Having self-knowledge and accepting your humanity is essential. The skill of intimacy is to share with others, not to set oneself apart. It's been my observation that newly ordained priests often fail to grasp this imperative, partly out of a desire to not make the same mistakes they've observed priests making in the past, especially in light of the sexual abuse scandals. They seem to believe that maintaining a distance from the laity is a prudent observance of boundaries that were lacking in the past. This is a well-intentioned but mistaken posture. You can't lead if you're distant. Who will follow? Being a priest or pastor means to engage in *intimate* communication: listening, identifying with, resonating (using your own emotional experience), clarifying (what do they mean?), formulating (using your knowledge and intellect), responding, and then leading.

Drawing again on the *Program for Priestly Formation*, "A person of affective maturity [is] someone whose life of feelings is in balance and integrated into thought and values; in other words, *a man of feelings who is not driven by them but freely lives his life enriched by them*" (emphasis added). For true intimate communication to occur, we need to allow ourselves to resonate, to *feel* what the other person is saying. This requires that we have access to our own wellspring of emotions. Over the years, I have found the most common problem among troubled clergy is poor emotional awareness. And that, in turn, allows insidious processes to get us into trouble. If we don't acknowledge feelings of loneliness, for example, how can we deal with them in a way that proves beneficial?

The Problem with "People Pleasing"

In contrast to differentiating themselves from the laity, some pastors have difficulty saying *no*. Unfortunately, these so-called "people pleasers" become so time-constrained they neglect their families, friends, hobbies (if they have any), even their spirituality. Social isolation is often the result. On the other hand, clergy who moderate their desire to please typically reserve time for their personal lives without feeling selfish or anxious about disappointing others.

What I've observed is that one's sense of being a "good" person may depend on acceptance by others—on whether one is meeting their needs as *they* judge it. Let me be clear here: If your self-worth depends on others liking you, you're in trouble. As previously mentioned, this means you're attempting to build your self-esteem on an external foundation, and when others don't get what they want, you feel distressed and worthless. Before long, you're developing problems with time management, fund management, and self-esteem.

One solution is learning to live and operate within a world of limits. Translation: instead of saying no to a parishioner, say, "I would love to be able to do that, but we don't have the time (or money or ability) right now." Time management is about saying to someone, "I have an appointment and can't speak to you now, but let's plan to get together this Friday when I can give you the time you deserve."

Managing Confrontation

Difficulties with confrontation is a universal problem among clergy. When confrontation is routinely avoided, passive-aggressive behavior can often take its place. Communication between a pastor and his associate or support staff may devolve into note writing, interpersonal avoidance, and building of resentment among both parties. Without the ability to manage confrontation, you lose the ability to manage yourself, your staff and other relationships, and interpersonal conflicts. In short, you are unable to collaborate.

All of which begs the question, How are you going to work with others if you cannot resolve conflict? It's naïve to assume that disagreements and misunderstandings won't occur when working with others. Confrontation is essentially a discrepancy between two or more people. Perhaps a staff member didn't perform as expected. Why, then, is this so hard to manage? What do we fear when we think of confronting someone? We fear we will hurt the other person's feelings or have our own feelings hurt. We fear angering the other person, leading to conflict and the raising of voices. We fear the other person won't like us anymore (a consequence of the aforementioned "people pleasing").

To give a practical example, on several occasions I've come across pastors who have had issues with secretaries they inherited from previous pastors. In one case, not only was the employee not very skilled, but she looked for opportunities to undermine the pastor because of her attachment to his predecessor. And because she had been at her job a long time—in fact, she practically ran the parish—the new pastor feared that firing her would touch off something of a palace revolt. In another case, the parish secretary had poor skills but was such a nice person the new pastor could never bring himself to hurt the employee's feelings.

The upshot? Both secretaries kept their jobs, but with a price. Because the authority of the first pastor was constantly undermined, he became more and more resentful. The second pastor was forced to correct his secretary's mistakes, which meant typing things himself, preparing the church bulletin, and doing other small tasks because it was just easier that way. Given how strapped pastors are for time, you can imagine how unhealthy and intolerable this situation became. Lack of conflict resolution came back to haunt both pastors.

How, then, do we confront people in a productive manner? There are some practical rules of the road. First of all, keep in mind the discrepancy is about the persons' actions, not about the persons. There is no need to apologize for anything you have said, or to be anguished you may have hurt their feelings. Instead, you should start by reminding them of your positive regard for them and their contribution to the parish. Next, calmly and clearly spell out the issue that divides you—what happened, what you thought was going to happen—working through the discrepancy in a logical way. Most important, discuss what your expectations are going forward. If they get upset, that is *their* issue, and you should not respond in kind. To do so would be to surrender control of your emotions to them. Instead, you have a responsibility to understand and clarify why they're upset.

You can start to see how skilled confrontation enables *friendship and collaboration.* It can actually be a relief to others—they now know where you stand and where they stand. When things are unclear, suspicion and anxiety ensue as negativity and fear fill the vacuum. Skillful confrontation is an opportunity for positive feelings and intimate communication.

Accepting Authority

Ask any chancery personnel director or bishop, and they'll tell you that priests who have difficulty with authority are a common problem. Typically, they have a chip on their shoulder or feel the need to constantly show who is "top dog." An aspect of this is "personalization"— the feeling that everything is a reflection on their worth and status. Another offshoot is to judge the behavior of others through a filter that sees conflict where none exists.

Let me assure you this is a lonely and angry place to be. A healthy priest is one who accepts the authority of others—within limits—to serve the good of the church and its people. The *Program for Priestly Formation* is again instructive here: "A person of affective maturity . . . [is] evidenced in his ability to live well with authority and in his ability to take direction from another, and to exercise authority well among his peers."

Keeping Social Isolation at Bay

Part of the difficulty of transitioning from the seminary to the "real world" is maintaining a social network. While that might have been easy in the seminary, it changes significantly in the parish, and is even more difficult when you become pastor. You are now in a position of power and living in a fishbowl. Spending time with one person or group, for example, can appear to be "playing favorites." There are new pressures and problems that daily demand your attention. As a result, socializing may seem like a waste of time and energy. Just closing your door, collapsing in your recliner, and having some time to yourself may seem far more desirable.

This is another "insidious" process (defined as one that causes harm in a way that is gradual and not easily noticed) lying in wait for pastors. Pretty soon people stop calling you because you are always busy—or maybe you stop returning their calls from the comfort of your recliner. If you find yourself on this treadmill, you have entered red-flag territory.

Needing friends is not a weakness. You are human, after all, and you need others to validate your existence. That's why your peers—other pastors and priests—are particularly important. They are supportive, caring, and help keep you in check. If you're having difficulty with an issue or an individual, you need to talk it over with others who understand the nuances and difficulties of your situation. Normally you can't do this with parishioners, for that would be to cede your role as their priest, serving instead as their friend. That is what *boundaries* are about.

Be aware that socializing with peers takes some planning. You already know this if you've tried calling priest friends at the last minute to see if they're available on your day off. They're probably not, which can lead to discouragement and social withdrawal. With a little advance planning, however, you can help ensure you're both free and able to enjoy a relaxing day away from the parish and all its attendant concerns.

Accepting Compliments

Does the following sound familiar? "I hear the one negative comment about my homily and dismiss the one hundred positive compliments— they're just being nice." Allowing in the positive is part of maintaining self-worth and avoiding false humility. Those who compliment you will instinctively know if you are not receptive to them. Not allowing such compliments in can lead you to pursuing affirmation in other, inappropriate ways, such as flirting or seeking adulation from parishioners.

Learn how to accept compliments. This is not about pride, but support. As the *Program for Priestly Formation* puts it, "A man of communion . . . [is] open to others and available to them with a generosity of spirit. The man of communion is capable of making a gift of himself and of receiving the gift of others."

Accenting the Positive

Like people in any field, priests who dwell on the negative aspects of work, relationships with others, and the world around them generally are destined for a life of misery and stress. As part of your emotional awareness development, ask yourself, Am I looking at the negative side only? What are the positives? Then engage a peer or friend in the discussion. Research shows that dwelling in life's dark and gloomy corners contributes to poor adjustment and early burnout. Furthermore, negative emotions can have a pervasive influence on perceptions and behaviors, so that potentially valuable resources like social and organizational support are never fully appreciated or utilized.

By shifting gears from "learned helplessness" to "learned optimism," the psychologist Martin Seligman developed a program to accentuate the positive. One of his techniques is to think of three good things at the end of each day and write them down in a journal. This exercise should be done during a prearranged quiet period in which you're able to listen to God and to your own heart, and reflect on the events of the day. There will be some days, of course, where things didn't go well but through a better understanding of *why*, you can make adjustments to ensure the next day is better. Keeping this kind of journal also encourages gratitude and an inner optimism.

I've had priests say to me, "That sounds nice, but I really don't have the time for it." My response to them is, "You owe it to yourself to take the time. If you realize how important it can be to your well-being, you'll find a way to make it happen."

Adjusting to the Priesthood

I've found through my work with priests that those who adjust best to their jobs have an ability to disengage from their demanding roles as leaders every minute of the day. In other words, those who take time to tend to their needs as human beings fare the best. It is not selfish to minister to oneself.[3]

Other traits that can help prevent burnout are a sense of personal autonomy, strong social support, and organizational backing. That's why having a mentor is extremely important. It's your acknowledgment that you can't do it all, that you don't (nor should you) have all the answers, that you don't believe seeking guidance is a sign of weakness.

It's amazing to me that so many priests don't have a spiritual director. We all instinctively know that an internal orientation to spirituality is essential to vocational satisfaction. The danger of not having that focus is for you to turn away from and sacrifice the ingredient that is most vital to your vocation: spirituality. Finding the right spiritual director is not always easy; in fact, it's becoming increasingly difficult. But given the multitude of pressures and distractions that priests confront daily, it's a task you can't afford *not* to undertake.

The Protective Effect of Self-Compassion

A heavy dose of self-compassion can also help ease your journey through priesthood. As discussed by the authors Laura Barnard and John Curry, it can benefit you in three ways. First, by offering you kindness, patience, and understanding during times of failure, stress, or disappointment. Second, by recognizing that others find themselves in similar valleys and by having self-compassion they are able to feel connected rather than isolated. Third, by allowing you to hold your worries in *mindful awareness* without ruminating on them you are free to dwell on positive accomplishments, rather than be brought down by emotional exhaustion.[4]

Essential to developing self-compassion is spending fifteen to twenty minutes in both the morning and the evening on contemplation (the evening portion could be your journaling exercise, previously discussed). These should be quiet periods in which you listen to God and to your own heart, and reflect on events of the most recent day, and the day that lies ahead.

The Importance of Physical Health

It's not uncommon for priests to eschew physical exercise on the following grounds: "Why should I selfishly spend time working out or caring for my own health? That's not serving the people." The answer, of course, is that if you want to have a long and successful priesthood, you need to take care of your physical self. Literature is replete with studies that demonstrate the stress-reducing and resilience-enhancing effects of exercise. To be in shape not only increases stamina but elevates mood. I know of a number of pastors who have undertaken exercise regimens and reaped tremendous benefits. These include extra stores of energy, motivation, and enthusiasm that bring them "faithfully" to the gym at five in the morning for their daily workouts.

Fighting Addiction through Active Coping

One way to think of addiction is as a compulsion designed to distract us from unpleasant and often painful perceptions of ourselves. It can encompass alcohol abuse, pornography, sex, gambling, overeating, and masturbation. Almost any activity can be done in a compulsive way (without awareness or conscious control) to achieve the goal of emotional denial.

To break the cycle of addiction, we need to adopt an *active* coping style and be able to access our interior lives. That means fighting social isolation and accepting the help of others. It means taking a spiritual "inventory" and discovering how and why we've become disconnected from our spiritual selves. We then need to apply and practice the skills that we've discussed—exercising self-compassion, accenting the positive in your life, accepting support from a mentor/ spiritual director/ social network, knowing how to disengage from your pastoral role every minute of the day, taking time for your physical needs—to get back on the right path.

You Owe It to Yourself

As you evolve in your spiritual role as pastor, it's important to recognize the need to grow in other ways as well. There are things you can—

and must—do to promote and ensure your wellness. As the *Program for Priestly Formation* points out, social interaction and skills should not be viewed as peripheral to what you do, but as integral to your vocation. By paying attention to and practicing self-care, you can lessen the likelihood of problems and pressures overwhelming you.

An active coping strategy embraces a host of things you can do for yourself to maintain a healthy mind and body. I suggest keeping a "Wellness Checklist," similar to the one that follows, to keep you focused in social, spiritual, pastoral, emotional, and physical realms.

Monthly Wellness Checklist

SOCIAL

1. ☐ I called a peer and made a social appointment for some time in the next two weeks.

2. ☐ I called a family member and caught up with the goings on in our family.

3. ☐ I spoke with a friend about my week. I listened to the positive and negative things my friend has been through as well.

4. ☐ I have been mindful of my boundaries with staff and parishioners.

5. ☐ I have been mindful of my feelings and fantasies.

6. ☐ I did not view inappropriate material on my computer this month.

SPIRITUAL

7. ☐ I celebrated Mass and prayed the Office.

8. ☐ I did some spiritual reading.

9. ☐ I prayed the rosary.

10. ☐ I have scheduled a meeting with my spiritual director/confessor within the next month or so.

11. ☐ I prepared for an upcoming day of recollection or annual retreat.

12. ☐ I spent some time before the Blessed Sacrament devoting myself to some one-on-one time with the Lord.

PASTORAL

13. ☐ I have tried to be mindful of my motivations for ministry—it is not in the service of being liked, admired, or adored.

14. ☐ I have been able to be compassionate and understanding with parishioners and staff, modeling "kindness" whenever I could.

15. ☐ I made a pastoral visit to a parishioner at home or in the hospital.

16. ☐ With compassion and nurturance, I was able to confront someone who needed it.

17. ☐ I maintained an attitude of collaboration with my staff.

EMOTIONAL

18. ☐ I maintained self-compassion.

19. ☐ I looked for, and let go of, resentment.

20. ☐ My mood has been positive; I feel hopeful about the future.

21. ☐ I have felt gratitude for friends and family.

22. ☐ I have been aware of my feelings and did not distract myself from them with work or avoidance.

23. ☐ I did not feel lonely; or, if I did, I tried reaching out to others.

24. ☐ I planned and protected my day off and spent it outside the rectory.

25. ☐ I have spent some good "alone" time, allowing myself to decompress and relax.

26. ☐ I have nurtured myself with some activity I enjoy, such as reading a book, watching a movie, focusing on a hobby, etc.

PHYSICAL

27. ☐ I have had a medical checkup within the last year and I am caring for my health by taking my medications and following my doctor's advice.

28. ☐ I did not abuse nicotine, alcohol, food, or other drugs.

29. ☐ I have done 20–30 minutes of daily exercise.

30. ☐ I watched my diet, and have been mindful of my weight.

Essentially, a pastor's wellness is a carefully balanced system, each facet feeding the others. That's why it's not a bad idea to sit down at the end of each day and take stock of what happened. It should be a quiet period in which you may listen to God and to your own heart and reflect on the events of the day.

I also suggest writing down three things that went well, and why. There will be some days that don't go well, of course. We've all had them, and there's nothing wrong with acknowledging it. But through a better understanding of why they occurred, we can take steps to ensure that the next day is sunnier, that we're better able to deal with the drumbeat of issues and the people around us from a position of confidence and strength.

I've had priests say to me, "Checklists and journals sound nice, but I just don't have the time." My response to them is, "You owe it to yourself to take the time. If you realize how critical it is to your well-being, you'll find a way to make it happen."

Endnotes

1. Pope Francis, Address to participants in the convention on the 50th anniversary of *Optatam Totius* and *Presbyterorum Ordinis*, November 20, 2015, Libreria Editrice Vaticana, https://w2.vatican.va/content/francesco/en/speeches/2015/november/documents/papa-francesco_20151120_formazione-sacerdoti.html.

2. United States Conference of Catholic Bishops, *Program of Priestly Formation*, 5th ed. (Washington, DC: USCCB, 2006), 76.

3. D. K. Pooler, "Pastors and Congregations at Risk: Insights from Role Identity Theory," *Pastoral Psychology* 60 (October 2011).

4. Laura Barnard and John Curry, "The Relationship of Clergy Burnout to Self-Compassion and Other Personality Dimensions," *Pastoral Psychology* 61, no. 2 (April 2012).

A Pastor's Pivotal Role in Strengthening Catholic Schools

John Eriksen

Despite the headline-grabbing facility closings of recent years, Catholic schools are experiencing a hopeful new period of ascendancy, which should prove heartening to new pastors and priests. To be sure, pastors now have a range of resources and tools at their fingertips that go well beyond what their predecessors could access. These include the laity who, equipped with diverse and powerful skill-sets, are becoming increasingly engaged in improving and growing Catholic schools in communities around the country. As the valuable contribution of religious and ordained to the Catholic school system continues to decline, the laity has stepped up to the plate in growing numbers to take on important roles in the operation and management of Catholic schools.

A second catalyst for positive change has been a rapid expansion of school choice programs in the form of tax credits, vouchers, and educational savings accounts. This growth has been driven in no small part by the Catholic Church's advocacy efforts on behalf of these progressive policies. As a result, twenty-eight states now have some form of school choice program, enabling thousands of families to benefit from a Catholic education. While there is still a long way to go nationally, these programs make a strong statement about the value and viability of Catholic schools in our society today.

Another encouraging sign is the array of organizations and universities—including the Cristo Rey Network, Seton Education Partners, and the University of Notre Dame's Alliance for Catholic Education (ACE) program—all of whose work is helping to create new Catholic schools, improve existing schools, and train new teachers and school leaders. Furthermore, dioceses from New York and Philadelphia to Minneapolis and San Jose have taken creative and proactive measures to strengthen their schools.

Reinforcement has also come from philanthropic organizations such as FADICA (Foundations and Donors Interested in Catholic Activities) and the Philanthropy Roundtable.[1] These groups have dedicated significant time and resources to Catholic schools, including the dissemination of literature that raises the visibility and extols the promise of Catholic school education in the United States.

For these reasons and many more, a pastor who is assigned to a parish with a Catholic school or one that is perhaps thinking of opening one need no longer have a sense of apprehension and foreboding. He can look to the future with optimism, knowing he can tap into a network of partners, tools, and resources prepared to help him effectively manage and grow his Catholic school enterprise.

Five Critical Tools and Resources for Pastors

Tool One: Advocacy

Among the most powerful tools for a pastor is advocacy, which he wields by simply conveying the importance of the Catholic school in his parish. There is no more forceful champion for advancing Catholic school education than a committed, passionate pastor. By evangelizing about the merits of Catholic schools within your parish, your deanery, and your diocese, you and other pastors like you send a truly powerful message that resonates nationally.

Even if you are a parish without a school, you can—and should—play the role of advocate. Your voice has the ability to benefit those parishes that do have schools and, on a much broader scale, to underscore the fact that Catholic education serves not just families within our own churches but vast numbers of underserved children in inner-city neighborhoods, thus relieving the public sector of that burden. That we've set high standards in the process is evidenced by the number of minority students who excel academically and have pursued higher education opportunities.

One crucial way to leave your mark as pastor is to advocate on behalf of school choice programs. Whether it's tax credits (where an individual or corporation makes a deductible gift), school vouchers (where the state directly funds a student's education at a Catholic school), or education savings accounts (think IRA or HSA, but for education), the public funding mechanisms to support Catholic schools today have increased significantly. Still, the beleaguered Catholic school system continues to fight a generations-old battle over its exclusion from public financing—a prohibition that is more untenable than ever in a modern-day context. Indeed, the United States is the only major industrial country that does not financially support private and faith-based schools. Behind this discriminatory practice are the Blaine Amendments—provisions in state constitutions that forbid the use of state funds for sectarian schools. Sadly, some thirty-seven states have these clauses in their constitutions, the products of bigotry designed to punish Catholics and Catholic works of charity.

Overcoming this obstacle by knowing about and being able to cite the unfairness of Blaine Amendments in many state constitutions is an advocacy tool that any pastor can effectively employ. The United States Catholic Conference of Bishops, your local Catholic Conference, and national organizations such as the American Federation for Children and the Friedman Foundation all provide useful resources and guidance for pastors and their parish communities.[2] Indeed, your emphasis should be not just on your own involvement but challenging your entire parish to help you become a vocal force for legislation allowing tax credits and other forms of religious education financing in states that prohibit them.

Tool Two: Skilled Support Network

A second critical tool (more a resource, really) for the pastor is his immediate support network—other pastors, principals, teachers, and the school's staff. With their experience and skill-sets, these professionals are well equipped to help you answer questions like, "Are we meeting the needs of our students?" and "What can we do to improve their educational experience?" Having multiple feedback loops and data gathering points to inform your decision making can prove invaluable.

Occasionally, I hear a pastor say he rarely seeks advice or counsel from others because they invariably have nothing new to add to the conversation. That's a narrow-minded and counterproductive attitude because even a discussion with no fresh ideas can serve to validate—or disqualify—a course of action on the pastor's part. There is always value in talking to others, even if it's not immediately apparent.

Another point that needs emphasizing is that your support network is not limited to those around you. Ready to help you meet challenges and capitalize on opportunities are organizations like Cristo Rey, Notre Dame's ACE, Seton Partners, NCEA, the Leadership Roundtable, and FADICA (which has produced a very useful school model catalogue).[3] Establishing an organized feedback loop within your Catholic school is integral to its success, and be aware that the Leadership Roundtable is particularly well equipped to help you with this process.

Tool Three: Recruiting Outside the System

A third tool for a pastor is recruiting talent from the rich pool that exists at the public school, charter school, and local college and university levels. This outreach could be directed particularly to individuals reared within the parish and Catholic school communities, and who would now welcome a job change that brings them back to their roots and reflects their beliefs. The pastor, for his part, should be relentless in connecting with and evangelizing these individuals about the professional, personal, and spiritual fulfillment that comes with working in the Catholic school system. As part of this effort, it doesn't hurt to ask other pastors, principals, and school administrators how they uncovered esteemed members of their leadership teams.

It bears mentioning here that for the past thirty years there has been some "bad blood" between Catholic schools and their charter school counterparts, often emanating from organizations and individuals associated with Catholic schools. This rift has been messaged in several ways. First, charter schools have been portrayed as "the competition" with a sinister ulterior motive, closing down Catholic schools, and, second, the donor community and policy leaders have somehow been hoodwinked into believing that *all* charter schools are good. My response is that, yes, charter schools are often in competition with Catholic schools, but that doesn't mean we can't learn from them. Remember, many charter school leaders have Catholic roots, or their school may actually be more "Catholic" than "charter." In my own experience I've found that many of these schools are willing to share what they have learned in terms of organization, culture, student interventions, and much more. In short, if you have a high-quality charter school nearby, you'd be well advised to pay it a visit and learn as much as you can about how it operates and how it educates students (the same can be said for visiting high-quality Catholic schools in your area).

I would also argue that many in the donor and policy communities are no longer exclusively Catholic school or charter school friendly. Instead, these communities are increasingly *kid friendly* and, as such, are looking for their resources to impact the greatest number of children in the most meaningful ways. Understanding this new dynamic is important for you as a pastor to unlocking each group's support.

A similar "us-them" mentality also exists around our historic relationship with public schools, though this has been somewhat easier for us to navigate because of the number of public school administrators and teachers who have transitioned between public and Catholic schools. Still, a residual jealousy exists on the part of some Catholic school educators over the resources public schools possess, and this, unfortunately, has served to diminish their effectiveness as professionals compared to their public school peers. In fairness, there are "bad" public school educators as surely as there are "bad" Catholic and charter school educators. That, however, is more the exception than the rule, and I've found a number of public school superintendents and school leaders who are quite friendly to Catholic schools and cling strongly to the belief that every child is entitled to a quality education regardless of the purveyor. I think a pastor who treats public and charter schools as mission-aligned colleagues and not as foes or competitors will invariably be better served. So when interacting with a public school or charter school principal, ask yourself, "What can I learn from this educator that will help *my* school community do a better job?"

Tool Four: Benchmarking

A fourth critical tool for pastors is benchmarking their school against others to determine if they are succeeding or falling short of the highest standards. This requires, first of all, defining "success" within today's Catholic school framework and then measuring their performance against schools that have been recognized as models. There are many exemplars of fidelity, clarity, and achievement to mission and a pastor should make the time to visit and observe these schools and continually ask, "Is my school living up to this standard?" A helpful strategy is to walk the halls and engage students, teachers, parents, and school leaders about their mission and vision and, most important, *why they are there*. It may seem obvious, but it's highly unlikely a Catholic school will be successful if all constituent groups don't understand why they are there and what they are supposed to be doing, or if they offer strikingly different answers to these questions.

Your principal should take the lead with this benchmarking effort. You should work in partnership with him or her, however, to identify the kinds of best practices that can lead to significant improvements in how you manage your own educational program.

Tool Five: Focus on Culture

A fifth tool or resource that I highly recommend is the book *Culture Eats Strategy for Lunch*, by Curt Coffman and Kathie Sorensen.[4] The title, attributed to management guru Peter Drucker, strongly makes the case that leaders often undervalue culture as a lever for success. I have seen this myself in many Catholic schools. Too often, pastors prioritize strategy over culture and enable this thinking among their principals and their entire parish school communities. Although *Culture Eats Strategy for Lunch* has secular connotations, it's also applicable to Catholic schools. Think about how you would respond if someone asked you questions like, "What is the culture of your Catholic school?" "Is it okay to make mistakes?" "Are school community members empowered to have open and frank conversations with one another about the strengths and weaknesses of your school?" "How does 'Catholicity' come alive within your school?"

Each of these questions directly relates to your school's culture. And while some may seem rather cliché, knowing where your school stands on each can have enormous long-term value. I've often found that Catholic schools, like schools in all sectors, get lazy or just assume they have the culture thing down pat. Parochial schools are particularly prone to this smugness and fail to understand the meaning and impact of culture trumping strategy.

Conclusion

This discussion has involved both "hard" and "soft" tools designed to help pastors, in partnership with educators, strengthen and grow their school systems. Regardless of the type of tool, an active and engaged pastor knows how to maximize each. The pastor who is an advocate for Catholic school education both in the parish and in the public policy arena is an invaluable asset to the entire church. Moreover, the pastor who expands his horizons and taps into the wealth of resources available within the educational ecosystem of the Catholic Church and other schools and organizations nationally is much better equipped for the kinds of decisions he must routinely make.

Finally, a pastor who understands the importance of culture—and is crystal clear about why the Catholic school is there and what it aims to accomplish, and who continually solicits feedback—positions himself and his school for sustainable success. Ten years ago I would not have written such a positive outlook about Catholic schools and the ability of pastors to help them weather the storm. Fortunately, that is no longer the case. As I've described here, the tools and resources exist and the timing has never been better for pastors to be leaders in the renaissance of Catholic schools.

Endnotes

1. See their websites: FADICA, http://www.fadica.org/main/; and Philan thropy Roundtable, http://www.philanthropyroundtable.org/.

2. See the website for the American Federation for Children, http://www .federationforchildren.org/; and the Friedman Foundation for Educational Choice, http://www.edchoice.org/.

3. To learn more about these organizations, visit their websites: Cristo Rey, http://www.cristoreynetwork.org/; Seton Partners, http://www.setonpartners .org/who-we-are/; Notre Dame's ACE (Alliance for Catholic Education), https://ace.nd.edu/about/the-alliance-for-catholic-education; the Leadership Roundtable (formerly the National Leadership Roundtable on Church Man-agement), http://leadershiproundtable.org/; and NCEA (National Catholic Educational Association), https://www.ncea.org/.

4. Curt Coffman and Kathie Sorensen, *Culture Eats Strategy for Lunch: The Secret to Extraordinary Results, Igniting the Passion Within* (Denver, CO: Liang Addison Press, 2013).

Leadership in Complex Pastoring Situations

Mark Mogilka

Parishes are changing dramatically. The one-pastor, one-parish model with a homogenous community of parishioners is becoming the exception. According to research published in 2011, 7 percent of all parishes in the United States are the product of a recent merger of two or more parishes, 27 percent share a pastor with at least one other parish, and 38 percent are considered multicultural.[1] Since this research was first published, these numbers have increased.

Clearly, these emerging parish models call for new forms of pastoral leadership. What I refer to as "complex parish pastoring"—spreading your time and talents among multiple parishes and multiple cultural communities—is more and more the rule rather than the exception. And your ability to learn new pastoral skills and adapt to these new parish realities will in large part determine your success as a pastor and a leader.

Adding to the complexity of changing parish models is the fact that the Catholic population will continue to grow, especially through the influx of Hispanics, while the number of priests will continue to decline. In recent years there have been questions raised by the Vatican over diocesan initiatives to close parishes. As a result, I believe that pastors will increasingly be asked to serve in even larger parishes, multiple parishes, and parishes that are more culturally diverse and, hence, more complex.

My hometown Diocese of Green Bay, Wisconsin, provides a good illustration of the rapidly changing landscape of the Catholic Church in America. In 1988, we had 219 parishes; today, we have 157. We've been through many parish reorganizations and changes. Fully 65 percent of our parishes now share a pastor with at least one other parish. In one case, we had a single pastor with responsibility for six parishes. In recent years we have also taken steps to meet the growing needs of the Hispanic community in the city of Green Bay. This community has doubled over the past decade to embrace at least 14 percent of all households in the city. Within our diocese, eight parishes are now engaged in special ministries with the Hispanic community. In addition, we have another seventeen parishes that, while single canonical parishes, have two or more churches that celebrate Mass each weekend.

To be effective pastors and leaders in complex pastoring situations, we need to begin by asking the basic question, How do we define, or what do we mean by, effective leadership? There are two parts. First is the ability to articulate a *vision*, to make God's dream a reality within the church. And second, leadership is the ability to *engage people* to make that vision a reality. We need to instill in parish leaders and parishioners a sense of ownership and a willingness to help bring God's vision to life. Both parts are essential. I know leaders who are great visionaries but don't know how to engage and motivate people to make those visions come true. Likewise, there are parishes that have engaged many people and are quite busy with activities but have no vision and aren't going anywhere. These shortcomings are magnified in complex pastoring situations.

Basic Vision

So, the first question on the road to being an effective leader of a complex parish setting is, *What's your vision of what a parish should be today?* In workshops that I've done with priests and with lay leaders around the country, I rarely get a common answer. It's obvious that we don't have a unified understanding of the modern-day basic vision for even a traditional parish, much less a complex parish. This raises an even more important question: How effective can we be as a church if pastors, lay leaders, and parishioners don't have a common understanding of why the parish exists?

There is an official answer to that question. It comes from the *Catechism of the Catholic Church*, paragraph 2179, which cites four parish building blocks. First, the parish is a community entrusted to a pastor as its shepherd. It is a web of relationships comprised of loving, caring people who support one another. Second, it's a place where the faithful gather for Eucharist, the sacraments, and worship. Third, it's a place where religious doctrine is taught and people are formed throughout their lives. Finally, the parish is a place where charity and good works are practiced.[2] Pope Francis has added a fifth building block: evangelization.[3]

So, when we talk about a vision for the modern-day parish, we should keep in mind these basic building blocks that should be reflected in any written parish mission statement. *How many of us have a parish mission statement?* Each parish should have a unique mission statement that reflects its basic vision. Unfortunately, most are long, rambling documents. My challenge to you is, consider boiling down your statement to fifteen to twenty words that can be easily remembered. At the very least, it should acknowledge that you are a community that celebrates the Eucharist, teaches Catholic doctrine, and practices charity, good works, and evangelization. To my mind, these elements should be at the core of any good parish mission statement.

Portrait of Today's Pastor

So if the vision is clear, what is the reality of how pastors spend their time? Research offers some insight, showing how the ever-growing complexity and diversification of parishes has reconfigured the role of pastor. Instead of being able to spend adequate time on your pastoral ministry—the reason most of you responded to God's call to serve—you're now required to spend more and more time on church administration. A study done in 2006 across various church denominations showed that priests, on average, work fifty-six hours per week. This was the most hours per week on average of any denomination in the country. Just as revealing, the study found that, on average, 31 percent of Catholic pastors' time is devoted to administering and attending meetings. On the other hand, Protestant pastors spend, on average, 14 percent of their time on administration.[4]

Clearly, there's something wrong with this picture. I'd like to suggest there are much better uses for your time than committing nearly a third of it to administration. It's helpful to look to the wisdom of Pope Benedict XVI on this matter. When asked at a meeting with Italian priests in July 2007 how they should handle their growing responsibilities, including ministering to multiple parishes, the Holy Father replied that their bishops "must see clearly how to ensure that the priest continues to be a pastor and does not become a holy bureaucrat." The Holy Father went on to state, "I think it very important to find the right ways to delegate . . . [and the priest] should be the one who holds the essential reins himself, but can rely on collaborators."[5]

Engaging People to Carry Out the Vision: Art of Delegating

Remember, good leaders articulate a vision but, just as important, they engage people to make the vision a reality. One of the most important tools for engaging people is through "delegating," as noted by Pope Benedict. It's one of the essential skill-sets that pastors—especially those in complex environments—need to actively cultivate. Unfortunately, there are a number of myths and misconceptions regarding delegating responsibilities. I'd like to address some of them.

First myth: *You can't trust employees and volunteers to be responsible.* Keep in mind that part of your job as a leader is to mentor and guide people to *be* responsible and call them to account. Here, your formation, background, training, and experience will serve you well.

Second myth: *When you delegate you lose control.* You need to learn how to delegate but not abdicate your responsibility. It is absolutely essential that you call on the people of God to use their gifts and talents in service to the community and delegate as much of the responsibility as is feasible. Otherwise, you fall into the common trap of "I'm the only one who can do it correctly." And that, I can assure you, is a one-way ticket to burnout. There is only so much you can accomplish by yourself. But with the assistance of others, incredible things are possible.

Third myth: *You can't fire a volunteer.* You certainly can and in some situations should. However, it should be done sensitively and discreetly, perhaps even couched in an invitation for them to use their gifts in a different aspect of ministry within the church.

Fourth myth: *If you delegate, volunteers will get the recognition you deserve for a job well done.* Remember, the most effective leaders are those who work in the background and celebrate the successes of those who are on their staff. Delegation actually increases your flexibility because it gives you more time to focus on your primary tasks of pastoring.

Fifth myth: *Your staff and volunteers are too busy to take on any more responsibilities.* Drawing on my own experience, I have a staff of seven and periodically fall into the trap of "Oh, they're working so hard I can't ask them to do one more thing." Sure you can. Usually, that means sitting down with them to figure out what work or project they can put aside to make room for the more urgent task you need them to do. After all, you're the one in charge.

Final myth: *Volunteers don't see the big picture.* Sometimes they don't, but isn't that your job?

What are the steps, then, to being a better delegator of responsibilities? Most important, you need to effectively communicate the task. Oftentimes, those lines break down, or they never existed, and that's when problems typically develop. You should be spending at least thirty to forty-five scheduled minutes a month, one-on-one with every member of your parish staff. Ask them, "What happened over the last month?" and "What's coming up in the month ahead?" It's also an opportunity to discuss with them any concerns you may have about their performance. These meetings also provide a means for you to be able to affirm and mentor them, and thereby help them in their ministry to the community or communities you serve.

Another critical step in assigning responsibilities is to delegate not just the task but the authority that staff members need to get the job done. Set the standards up front as well as your expectations of what should be done. Also, be sure to give them the background information they need and offer your full support and commitment.

Sometimes we delegate a task and come back six months later to find out the staff member or volunteer hasn't even begun the project because of other priorities. That's a sign that you haven't been a very good delegator. You should have established up front the time frame for completing the task, and then followed up at least once a month to determine what progress has been made toward that goal.

Last but not least, provide affirmation for a project well done. And when a project isn't well done, ask the question, "What did you learn?"

Engaging Laypeople

In complex pastoring situations, being a successful pastoral leader and good delegator also means you've come to accept the importance of the laity in fulfilling your role as pastor. According to the Code of Canon Law, the pastor as shepherd "carries out the functions of teaching, sanctifying, and governing, also with the cooperation of other presbyters or deacons and with the *assistance of lay members of the Christian faithful*" (c. 519, emphasis added).

Part of the framework of being a great pastor today, especially in complex pastoring situations, is engaging laypeople. In the document *Ecclesia in America* (1999), Pope St. John Paul II was even more explicit: "A renewed parish needs the collaboration of laypeople and therefore a director of pastoral activity and a pastor who is able to work with others" (41). I'm always amazed that we haven't more fully mined this pearl of wisdom from St. John Paul. In today's environment, effective leadership means finding people who can complement your gifts as pastor.

Building Bridges among Parish Communities

Given the complex pastoring situations you find yourself in, articulating a vision for multiple communities or cultures has never been more challenging. Here again, John Paul II had some helpful advice. "One way of renewing parishes," he suggested, "might be to consider the parish as a community of communities and movements" (*Ecclesia in America* 41). This vision has more recently been articulated by the USCCB Committee on Cultural Diversity in the 2013 publication *Best Practices for Shared Parishes: So That They May All Be One.*

What do we mean by "community of communities"? Implicit in this phrase is the ability to recognize and affirm the unique characteristics of each community within each parish, and the unique communities within each single parish, especially in multicultural situations. This requires you to directly address two questions. First, what are my vision, hopes, and dreams for my parish or parishes as a whole? And second, what are my vision, hopes, and dreams for each individual parish or community within a single parish?

In your articulation of the vision for each individual community and the broader community, it is critical to engage key leaders from each separate community. As part of that process, it's important to find out who are the key drivers and thought leaders within these communities, and how do I build relationships with them? Remember that each community, each ethnic group, has a unique leadership style, a unique way of coming to the table, and a unique way of getting things done.

There are three basic models to keep in mind when building bridges among diverse parish communities: coexistence, collaboration, and consolidation. Each has its unique challenges and opportunities. In the case of coexistence, separate communities are members of the same church and may share the same worship space, but that's usually where the commonality ends. There is little interaction between them; they're virtual silos. The second model is collaboration. Here, communities maintain their basic identities but also have areas of overlap that you can build on. For example, there may be several annual events—like the parish festival or Christmas program—that bring all parishioners together and can serve as a springboard for partnerships in other areas, like fund-raising and outreach. The third model is consolidation, or merger, where communities come together as a seamless whole. It's a nice ideal, but since the roots of one's primary community tend to be especially deep, a true merger of diverse communities rarely happens.

Regardless of the model that defines your parish, you should be aware of the ways in which communities can cooperate. There will always be some parish cultures and ethnic cultures that can be quite compatible and blend together nicely. Others, however, maintain strong boundaries and are resistant to consolidation. It's important for you as pastor to realistically assess what the prospects for cooperation and collaboration are. As noted by the US Conference of Catholic Bishops, when dealing with diverse communities the goal is not assimilation, but *inclusion*.[6] Don't frustrate yourself by setting up unrealistic expectations to create "unity" in the face of deeply committed and tightly bound communities that simply are not able to come together.

What are some of the variables that determine how compatible parish communities and multicultural communities within a diverse parish can be? They include ethnic identity, ecclesial identity and practices, relative size, economic health, geography, decision-making processes, parish program priorities, staff, parishioner involvement, tolerance for change, and parish viability.

Your overarching goal when managing a complex parish environment should be to create a wonderful community of communities—a beautiful new mosaic—and not necessarily a melting pot. To accomplish this, you need to come to grips with three fundamental questions:

- What do these communities share in common that you can build on?

- What's unique and special in each community that must be acknowledged, honored, and respected?

- What's the best way to provide pastoral leadership to each community within this mosaic?

In responding to these questions, never lose sight of the fact that change—external change that you can see and touch—is easy; but transition—changing people's hearts, attitudes, beliefs, and values—takes a lot more time and patience. Many would suggest this kind of change, or coming together, literally takes generations.

A recent look at the field of social psychology has provided some new insights on how to foster unity between and among diverse groups. The first insight is to not declare it as your goal, because that just triggers resistance and the "circling of the wagons" to fend off any change or loss of identity. Instead, pastoral leaders should affirm diverse groups and help them to learn how to work together on important projects. As they work together, they build relationships. The relationships break down barriers between them. Their joint accomplishments provide them with a shared sense of pride and a new identity, and over time help to foster unity.

Multi-Parish Pastoring

It is important to note that when comparing traditional parishes to multi-parish ministries, research shows there is little or no difference when it comes to parishioner and leader evaluations of overall satisfaction and their evaluation of the quality of ministries and services provided by the parishes.[7]

Multi-parish pastoring does have its own set of distinct challenges. The biggest of these, according to research, is lack of time. More specifically, how do you manage your private time, scheduling complexities, and drive time between parishes? Just as significantly, how do you use the limited time you *do* have to best advantage, knowing you can't possibly be in as many places as you want, or need, to be.

The second greatest challenge, research shows, is attempting to manage multiple parishes where there is little discernible cooperation or collaboration among its diverse communities, or where parishioners feel you favor the other parish and don't spend enough time with them. These may seem like petty matters, but to parishioners they're very real.

Third on the list of challenges for multi-parish pastors is finding replacement help for days off, vacations, retreats, and service days outside the parish. This challenge can easily throw you into the guilt trap of not taking days off.

Finally—and not unrelated—is the challenge of serving small parishes with their limited staffing and resources.[8]

While the challenges of multiple-parish pastoring are very real, there is a growing body of research, best practices, and organizational models that can be a great help to pastors and parish leaders who serve in multiple-parish ministry situations.[9] Multi-parish ministry should not be seen as a problem to be solved or avoided, but a model with unique opportunities for the sharing of gifts and talents among communities that need to be further developed.[10]

In the Diocese of Green Bay, we've seen firsthand how complex the parish—and the ministry of pastoring—have become. Beware of self-fulfilling prophecies. If you believe that navigating your way through diverse cultures and multiple parishes, while managing your time effectively, has made your job more difficult, if not burdensome, then it probably will be just that. On the other hand, if you view complex pastoring as an opportunity to be stretched—to orchestrate diverse unique gifts and talents into the creation of a beautiful mosaic—then you will find your ministry more stimulating and rewarding. God be with you and bless you in your efforts.

Endnotes

1. Mark Gray, Mary Gautier, and Melissa Cidade, *The Changing Face of U.S. Catholic Parishes*, Emerging Models of Pastoral Leadership CARA report (Washington, DC: NALM, 2011).

2. *Catechism of the Catholic Church*, 2nd ed. (United States Catholic Conference—Libreria Editrice Vaticana, 1997).

3. Pope Francis, *Evangelii Gaudium* (The Joy of the Gospel), 2013.

4. Jackson W. Carroll, *God's Potters* (Grand Rapids, MI: Eerdmans, 2006).

5. "Meeting with Italian Priests," *Origins* 37, no. 12 (August 30, 2007).

6. Committee on Cultural Diversity, *Building Intercultural Competence for Ministers* (USCCB, 2012).

7. Emerging Models of Pastoral Leadership, CARA studies and reports, 2011 and 2012.

8. Katarina Schuth, *Priestly Ministry in Multiple Parishes* (Collegeville, MN: Liturgical Press, 2006).

9. Mark Mogilka and Kate Wiskus, *Pastoring Multiple Parishes* (Chicago: Loyola Press, 2009).

10. Emerging Models, CARA, 2011, 2012.

Intercultural Competence for Ministry: Mapping the Road Ahead

Allan Figueroa Deck, SJ

For a book purporting to be a "toolbox," that is, a practical resource for engaging complex challenges with handy and accessible aids for remedying the situation, this chapter may seem at first rather theoretical. All I can say is that I am a big believer in what some wise person said long ago: "Nothing is more practical than a *good* theory." Intercultural competence needs to be addressed from a more penetrating and comprehensive theoretical *and* practical perspective because what is at stake, really, is a deeper grasp of the Catholic Church's very identity and mission, one that goes beyond mere pragmatism. It is about what we do, but also about what we become and are! The reality of globalization, migrations, commerce, communications, and the struggle for human dignity has implications for the most basic units of the Christian community today—for each Christian individually as well as for the family, parish, diocese, apostolic movement, school, or Catholic organization. Hence mind-sets, heart-sets, and skill-sets in intercultural encounter have become increasingly indispensable for life, work, and ministry in today's world and church. Both domestically and globally, matters of war and peace, communications, travel, migration, and business are bringing people and their cultures together as never before in human history.

The Catholic Church is surely no stranger to this worldwide development. While at times throughout history Catholics have not paid attention to their own preaching by falling into ethnocentrism and racism, overall the church has been and is today more than ever a pioneer in intercultural sensibility. The very term "catholic" refers precisely to the church's mission to include all humanity in the loving embrace of a merciful God who desires to reach out to the ends of the earth in a relentless drive to *include* all rather than *exclude* anyone. Two millennia ago at one of the most critical moments in the fledgling church's history, St. Paul the apostle argued that the Gospel message and membership in the Christian community were open to all and that to be a follower of Jesus Christ did not require subscribing to Jewish norms and customs nor to those of any other culture. The Christian community was fundamentally open to all as a result of God's *universal love* and the *radical equality of all believers* in and through baptism. Hence the life of the church at all levels—family, parish, diocese, regionally or universally— has always been characterized by *a negotiation of differences*, giving and receiving, from among the myriad cultures and ways of being, thinking, feeling, and acting of a people. Moreover, this outgoing, inclusive understanding of the church's identity and mission captures the essence of the stunning program of ecclesial reform spearheaded by Pope Francis from the very start of his amazing pontificate. At the heart of it is the Holy Father's invitation to renew the church and the world by building cultures of encounter and dialogue.

After all, openness to culture in all its manifestations and emphasis on dialogue were signature features of the Second Vatican Council, as well as of the refreshing reforms being carried out today by Pope Francis in the spirit of that council fifty years after its closing. Moreover, the recognition of cultural diversity and intercultural effectiveness became priority concerns for the US church that the bishops directly confronted and affirmed when they established in 2008 the Secretariat of Cultural Diversity, for which I served as first executive director. These learnings and reflections flow directly from my experience of the secretariat in its early years.

Within four years of the establishment of the secretariat two important developments occurred: (1) the Cultural Diversity Network Convocation took place at the University of Notre Dame in 2010, and (2) coming on the heels of the convocation, a five-module workshop titled *Building Intercultural Competence for Ministers* (BICM) was published and disseminated in 2012. Practical lessons are waiting to be learned by paying attention to the experiences, methods, and contents of these two groundbreaking events. That is why in the remainder of this chapter I propose to review the more salient takeaways from the Notre Dame Convocation and from the five modules that constitute the BICM workshop because they afford insights into what intercultural competence is all about, map out the territory to be explored, and offer many practical lessons. I will highlight features of these experiences and resources that may be replicated or adapted to the growing number of diverse pastoral and organizational situations found in parishes and dioceses, as well as in Catholic schools, organizations, and apostolic movements. Hopefully, those looking for practical tools or at least suggestions will find something of value.

Lessons from the Cultural Diversity Network Convocation

The Notre Dame University gathering brought together a select group of five hundred leaders—laity, religious, and clergy, including several bishops—from six major families of US Catholics: European Americans, Hispanics/Latinos, African Americans, Asian and Pacific Islanders, Native Americans, and migrants, refugees and travelers. In designing the process, a broad base of participants was invited to give input by means of (a) initial, nationwide consultations with bishops and with existing leadership groups among the six communities identified and (b) informal surveys of leaders in the field, that is, in shared or multicultural parishes, diocesan offices, schools, seminaries, and Catholic organizations. In assuming leadership in planning the convocation, however, the Secretariat of Cultural Diversity had to overcome a serious obstacle to credibility. Many of the diverse communities perceived the very creation of the secretariat as an instance of a questionable emphasis on "multiculturalism." Let me explain.

The secretariat had come about as the result of merging longstanding secretariats, one for Hispanic Affairs and the other for African American Affairs. The new secretariat merged those two secretariats and added three other major communities to its purview—Native Americans, Asian and Pacific Islanders, and migrants, refugees and travelers. A serious and often legitimate criticism of this "multicultural" approach is that it short-circuits the need for the parish, diocese, or organization to establish and maintain *credibility* with the base of these diverse communities. Each cultural group needs its own space to pull itself together in contexts where it has sometimes or even often been neglected, overlooked, powerless, or discriminated against. As a result, there is a necessary role for what some call silos—spaces where distinct groups feel comfortable and can process their concerns and build up the necessary experience to engage the wider ecclesial and social reality *from a position of strength* rather than powerlessness. Unity in the church, after all, does not fall down miraculously from the sky. It happens as a result of much prayer and hard work: attitudes, knowledge, and skills that create communion out of the many differences of language, culture, social class, and other forms of diversity so characteristic of our times. In creating the Secretariat for Cultural Diversity at the USCCB, the Catholic bishops made a prudential judgment that time was ripe to move to a *second moment* in the realization of communion in diversity. This required bringing credible leaders of the diverse communities into real dialogue (give and take) among themselves and with the bishops and their representatives, and maintaining this dynamic among all parties concerned. One of the benefits of moving to this second moment in building up ecclesial communion is the opportunity for all participants to grow in attitudes, knowledge, and skills that support a deepening sense of mutual respect and trust.

A second source of criticism and concern regarding the drive toward "multiculturalism" is that it undercuts the urgent need to identify and raise up credible leaders from the respective ethnic/racial groups. Instead of having its own proper leaders recognized, persons from other groups are often raised up to leadership of these multicultural organizational units. No matter how well-intentioned these leaders may be, they are unable to serve as *role models* to encourage more leadership development in each diverse community. Echoing some of the same concerns noted here, the US bishops' Committee on Hispanic Affairs cogently voiced the ongoing concern about a mistaken multicultural way of thinking, as well as of a "one-size-fits-all" mind-set in their 2002 document titled "Encuentro and Mission: A Renewed Pastoral Framework for Hispanic Ministry."

Participants in the symposium spoke with concern about a "multicultural" model that consolidates minorities under one office, which is headed by a coordinator. In the experience of the participants, this model often dilutes the identity and vision of Hispanic ministry and those of other ethnic ministries. It can reduce effectiveness in dioceses, parishes, and Catholic organizations and institutions. The leadership in Hispanic ministry is particularly concerned about the reduction of resources and the limited access to the bishop that can follow the establishment of multicultural offices. Also expressed was concern about exclusion of Hispanic ministry from the decision-making process, particularly in the areas of budgets, plans, and programs specific to Hispanic ministry and its impact on other ministerial areas and in the mission of the church as a whole.[1]

In the same document, Hispanic ministry leaders note that the purpose of multiculturalism is to promote integration and unity among the diverse cultural groups in church and society. As such, multiculturalism is certainly a positive and necessary development. Yet the committee notes,

> Multiculturalism . . . has been critiqued for abetting a "one-size-fits-all" mentality in pastoral ministry by creating a situation in which all groups are put into the same basket. This can have a negative effect on diverse communities by depriving them of the exercise of subsidiarity and of opportunities to form their own leaders and develop appropriate pastoral and educational models, resources and initiatives.[2]

Another criticism of multiculturalism came from the African American community, which noted that emphasis on cultures can eclipse or erode awareness of *racism* which, despite real gains of the civil rights movement of the 1960s and '70s, continues to be a reality and matter of serious concern to the church and society. For all these reasons, then, a troublesome level of discomfort and uneasiness among the various ecclesial leaders of the diverse cultural and racial groups had to be reduced, if not eliminated, if the convocation process was to enjoy an adequate level of credibility among all concerned. The path forward, therefore, required those charged with initiating the process, that is, the Secretariat of Cultural Diversity, to demonstrate as much as possible an openness to every racial/ethnic community, an ability to listen, learn, and model intercultural effectiveness and mutuality at each step of the way.

Something that contributed mightily to the creation of a sense of mutual regard among the diverse groups was the diverse composition and planning of the Notre Dame Convocation's steering committee. Perhaps even more consequential was the composition of the committee on prayer and worship. It was essential that the various groups truly see themselves in the convocation's program of prayer and worship, since this would set the tone for everything else. Much thought was given to this and, consequently, among the participants on the committee were excellent Latino, African American, Asian, Native American, and European

American liturgists and musicians who knew from real-life experience how to blend elements of the church's sacred liturgy with rituals, symbols, and narratives of the diverse communities, and do so in a respectful, integral, beautiful, and inspiring way.

Perhaps the single most effective method used at the very outset of the encounter was *storytelling*. Each cultural group, including the European American or Anglo, as it is sometimes called, was asked to reflect on its particular Catholic heritage and express how it lives its Catholicism through rituals, symbols, and narratives special to it. Something very interesting occurred when the groups went off to discuss their particular ways of being Catholic, of bringing faith and church teaching to life. The various non-European groups, including the African Americans, went at it with gusto and found great joy and pride in reviewing their customs and distinctive styles of Catholicism.

If truth be told, however, the European American white group was a bit stumped. The task seemed somewhat awkward or strange to them for a couple of reasons. First, because the European Americans were simply used to thinking of their way of being Catholic as virtually the only way, they were the "insiders," as it were, and the other cultural groups were the "outsiders." This in itself was a revelation for the European American group, which discovered that the convocation process did not simply assume that the US way of doing things was *the* norm, much less the only way to proceed, but simply *a* norm in a church that *de facto* is a communion of diversity. The European Americans discovered what it's like to *level the field* by becoming simply one group among many. The experience of being an outsider can be a revelation. Perhaps another reason for some European American participants feeling "stretched" by the experience was that US Catholicism is very driven by the enforcement of standards. It is a very post-Tridentine Catholicism that may suffer from rigidity and from too much organization, standardization, and concern with rules. Many other forms of Catholicism lived by persons of other cultures are more spontaneous and *expressive*. They bring a rich aesthetic orientation, imagination, color, movement, affectivity, and sense of celebration to their Catholicism. Tendencies toward rigidity and inflexibility—what Bishop Robert Barron calls "beigeness"—hold some forms of Catholicism back from achieving a truly *inculturated evangelization*, which goes well beyond simply engaging the mind or keeping the rules.

Thus the promotion of intercultural competencies has everything to do with bringing the faith to life, giving real traction to what we believe by expressing it in captivating stories, gestures, rituals, and symbols instead of reducing it to the banality of standard norms and practices in the name of order or orthodoxy—what Pope Francis calls "turning the church into a tidy museum."

A practical question that arose during the convocation had to do with the need for every parish, diocese, school, and organization to ask how willing it was to treat "outside" cultures with respect and even mutuality. Without doing so, one does not get to first base in intercultural relations. It has been observed that sometimes a genuine sense of hospitality in Catholic parishes is only skin deep. People say "welcome," but they place a serious condition on it, namely, that the newcomers fit in and conform to the host community's way of doing things, to their social class sensibilities or other distinctions. True interculturality and hospitality in a Christian sense, at least, requires real openness to the *other* based on love and an ability to both *give* to others and *receive* from what they have to offer. It is not merely a matter of tolerance or "going along in order to get along." This realization marked the interaction among all the cultural groups to a notable degree at the convocation.

Mapping the Road to Intercultural Competence: What to Do

The first part of this chapter has tried to convey the idea that growth in intercultural competence requires careful thought and planning, but most especially a *change of attitude*. Responding to diversity in one's parish or in the diocese is not just a matter of "being nice" to others or engaging in a kind of hospitality that is skin deep. This second part outlines specific strategies and activities that are deeply *challenging* because they promote growth in cognitive, affective, and behavioral skills and characteristics that support effective and appropriate interaction in various cultural contexts. Yes, they require change in mind-sets and approaches to ministry in the concrete situations in which ministry is carried out. Some of these recommendations are general, others more specific, but all of them require imagination and an ability to take risks, or what Pope Francis likes to call "going out," leaving the security of the sacristy for the dangers of the street and risk "getting into an accident."

One place to begin is by simply formulating, reflecting on, and sharing answers about key questions that affect the depth and quality of the individual or collective response to the challenges of intercultural encounters. The space limits of this chapter do not allow me to fully develop these suggestions for action, but they do provide an opportunity to highlight at least some of the contents and practical methods found in the above-mentioned USCCB's BICM workshop. First, I will look at the all-important question of attitude—what has been called *heart-set*. Second, I will outline what kind of knowledge or *mind-set* must be acquired and enhanced. And third, I will profile some practical skills or *skill-sets* required for intercultural effectiveness. These three categories provide the *analytic tools* for properly assessing what to do, where to start, and where one wants to go in the development of intercultural sensibility.

Developing the Right Attitudes

1. *Curiosity*: The literature on intercultural competence insists that one of the more important attitudes necessary to engage others, *any* others, is curiosity. Strange as it may sound, efforts to develop intercultural capacities rise and fall on this. Without a true desire to *experience and know the reality of the other*, efforts to reach out in any form are "dead in the water." The sad truth is that some people simply lack curiosity and hence they remain locked in self-referentiality and, let me use the proper word, *ignorance*. (My father used to say, "Ignorance is bliss!") In a world of rising diversity there are many who cannot bear the cost of reaching out for various reasons. This heart-set must be cultivated if the parish, diocese, or wider church is ever to become a real force for evangelization.

2. *Bias, prejudice, stereotypes, and racism*: Here are four complicated attitudes or ways of feeling and thinking that create often insurmountable obstacles and effectively cut people off from one another. These deadly orientations are often, if not usually, held by people in an unconscious and unanalyzed way. Strange as it may sound, the more religious people are, the more imbedded these negativities can be. Module 4 of BICM develops this theme and provides simple group activities that will help ministers identify and moderate these deeply rooted but toxic tendencies in all human beings. These attitudes are perpetual "elephants in our ecclesial living rooms." One of the first attitudes that must be

overcome is the one that suggests that because we are a church community of faithful, good Christians, such negative tendencies could not possibly be found in us. Yet the recognition of these negative tendencies is so important for the Christian community at all times and places because it puts flesh and bones onto our assertion about the reality of our own personal sinfulness and how sin functions structurally as well in the church as an institution, and also in civil society.

3. *Living with ambiguity*: It goes without saying that exposure to the reality of cultural differences means confronting the fact that human beings deal with all kinds of important life situations in a variety of ways that may even seem strange and puzzling. People usually want clear and straight answers and are uncomfortable with whatever is different or *other*. Differences of language, race, culture, political ideology, and social class often elicit fear. Cultural competence requires an ability to live with these fears and strangeness—it comes with the territory—in a global church and world. Unity in the parish or church is not the result of denying or rejecting these differences, but of working through them to achieve communion in *diversity* rather than communion in *conformity*.

Developing Our Knowledge

1. *Culture*: Understanding what is meant by culture is the single most important key for grasping the church's contemporary understanding of its identity and mission today. Too many good Catholics, including some church leaders, seem to be challenged by the anthropological conception of culture as "the way of thinking, feeling, and acting shared by a people." Understanding religion depends on understanding culture because culture is "the way we human beings are who and what we are." At the heart of this idea of culture are stories, rituals, and symbols that are the powerful *building blocks of meaning* in people's lives. Module 2 of BICM provides a handy overview of this foundational bit of knowledge for appreciating why insight into cultures and how they work is so essential to *inculturated evangelization*—the church's mission.

In addition to the broad concept of culture, however, intercultural sensibilities require a deeper knowledge of how diverse cultures think about themselves and the world around them. For instance, do they take a *collectivist* or an *individualist* approach to human experience? Are they more feminine or masculine in how they approach experience and decision making? Do they prize hierarchy or "pecking orders," or do they prefer egalitarian arrangements that level differences among generations, genders, rich and poor, and so forth? Another defining characteristic of cultures is whether they exhibit and honor the customs and norms of the community's past, of ancestors. Or are they modern or postmodern, future-oriented and unaware or unconcerned about preserving values from the past? How do diverse cultures relate to time? Is punctuality valued or are relationships so important that they trump punctuality?

2. *Immersion and language experiences*: Finally, a knowledge of other cultures, languages, and religions learned by formal study or personal encounters is important. Personal experience—often as the result of taking risks—is the most important way to grow in intercultural sensibility. *Immersion experiences*, for example, can be gained by travel within or outside the United States but also by careful attention to the places where diverse cultures thrive right next door to us in virtually all US metropolitan and suburban centers. Neither the territoriality of the parish or diocese nor the limited audience of Catholic schools, organizations, and movements exonerates any of those particular units of the church from the mission to reach out and be as inclusive as possible.

Developing Skills

1. *Communication skills*: Effective communication demands that one truly know the one being addressed. One must know, for instance, whether the person or group being addressed belongs to an individualist or a collectivist culture. Even more pertinent is what happens when an individualist culture like that of the United States encounters collectivist cultures like those of Asia, Africa, and Latin America. The individualist culture sees life as a process of advancement for the individual person, while collectivist cultures see life as a matter of advancing the well-being of the family and community, not the individual. Time does not allow me to go into all the profound differences between these two types of cultures. The BICM workshop provides a more comprehensive view. Suffice it here to say that ignorance of these differences can lead to huge mistakes by pastors and lay ministers, along with failures to effectively communicate, persuade, and lead.

2. *Face management*: Flowing from the differences between collectivist and individualist cultures is the matter of "face." Saving face is a major concern in many Asian as well as other traditional cultures like

African and Latin American. This involves attitudes toward elders and ancestors as well as toward hierarchy and authority. Matters of gender relations may also be part of this. Intercultural sensibility demands a basic level of exposure to and insight about how all these complex cultural sensibilities function and interact in today's world.

3. *Conducting meetings/reaching decisions*: Involved here are conflicting attitudes toward the purpose of meetings. Traditional cultures do not think of them primarily as "getting something done." Rather, meetings are mainly about the cultivation of human relationships *for their own sake*. This is the contrast between cultures that stress *doing* (our modern and postmodern developed world) and others that focus on *being*. This is not a matter of right or wrong; it is simply about differences. In decision making, modern cultures tend toward a *democratic*, "take a vote and the majority wins," approach, while many collectivist, traditional cultures prefer a *consensus* approach that seeks to leave no one out.

4. *Leadership and conflict resolution*: In modern, individualist cultures, leaders are chosen because they can "get things done." In some collectivist cultures they are chosen because of the *relationship* they have by reason of age or family heritage, rank or status. Approaches to conflict vary from individualist to collectivist cultures. Individualist cultures see conflicts in terms of issues and seek to address differences directly. Collectivist cultures look first to relationships, not issues, because the most desired outcome is not resolving some issue or other, but maintaining good group face. Hence, being direct in one's communication can be inappropriate and ineffective.

Conclusion

Navigating the complex reality of cultures is not only, or mainly, a matter of skills but also of attitude and spirituality. One needs to be *converted* to the reality of the other, one needs to truly be motivated. Pope Francis is doing his part with his revolution, shaking things up with his calls for an *inclusive* rather than an exclusive church, one that always reaches out to others. But such outreach has consequences. Among them is the need to do our homework and get to work. These pages have focused on analytical tools and a few practical suggestions on how to go about doing that.

The culture of encounter and dialogue proposed by Pope Francis is as old as the Gospel itself. Our frisky Argentine pope did not invent the idea of the absolute centrality of encounter and dialogue for the well-being of the church. These realities have everything to do with the trinitarian, incarnate God we have come to know in Jesus of Nazareth. At this moment in human history, the Catholic Church, precisely because it is "catholic," is being invited and challenged as never before by this pope "from the ends of the earth" to pay witness to God's universal love by modeling intercultural sensibility and competence. The conditions are more than ripe for doing this. The Catholic Church in the United States has a privileged role in responding to this challenge, given the historic openness to immigrants and refugees that is one of the deepest and most authentic currents of both our Catholic and American identities.

Endnotes

1. "Encuentro and Mission: A Renewed Pastoral Framework for Hispanic Ministry," in *A New Beginning: Hispanic/Latino Ministry—Past, Present, Future* (Washington, DC: USCCB, 2012), 69.

2. *Building Intercultural Competence for Ministers* (Washington, DC: USCCB, 2012), 42. Another excellent resource is *Best Practices for Shared Parishes: So That They May All Be One* (Washington, DC: USCCB, 2013).

A Word about Managing Change:
From Readiness to Implementation

Dennis Cheesebrow

For new pastors, few roles are more daunting than acting as a change agent for their parishes. Great expectations recede as reality sets in. They discover that change happens slowly, encountering resistance from many quarters. The failures tend to be remembered more than the successes, the pain more than the joy.

As a pastor you know instinctively that change is needed. The good news is that through enlightened leadership on your part improvements can—and will—occur. The skills needed to effectively manage change across your parish can be learned, and the enabling tools and practices are known quantities. So let's look at how you can put these resources to work to guide change from readiness to implementation.

The Pastor-Staff-Parishioner Collaboration

The mission of the Catholic Church is delivered through the dynamic relationship between parishioner, pastor, and staff/volunteer. Any new parish pastoral plan, initiative, or change in practices should be implemented through this collaborative relationship. A pastor can choose to assert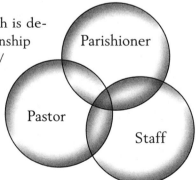

his authority and bypass that union, of course, but it's usually ill-advised and unproductive.

The Importance of Mission-Delivery Relationships

Positive change is possible when relationships are strong and respectful; it's difficult, if not impossible, when they are weak, disrespectful, and insular. The change leader is the pastor and by encouraging the development of mission-delivery relationships he creates an environment in which change can flourish. The mission-delivery point is the intersection of the three circles in the image above. When pastor, staff, and parishioners are clear about (1) the purpose or mission of the Catholic Church, (2) the vision of how it's carried out at the local parish, and (3) the shared outcomes, experiences, and goals that demonstrate everyone is on the same path to that vision, then they can better engage in a relationship of collaborative ministry and service.

Interestingly, as a parish moves toward meaningful improvements, voices of dissatisfaction will typically be raised. Parish leaders, for example, may balk at any changes in ministry that they've created over the years. Even diocesan-led changes may be viewed as unwanted or threatening. It's important to remember, however, that constructive criticism should not be discouraged but welcomed and respected, and woven into the process of change. It should be a natural part of both change readiness and implementation.

Tools and Practices for Guiding Change

Data, Research, and Analysis

These are valuable tools that can help you to build a strong case for change within your parish, bolstered by the anticipated results. Data, research, and analysis provide an objective balance to human input, allowing the pastor and parish leaders to see the bigger picture and take a more systemic view of growth and change. Dioceses can often provide these information-based resources to pastors and parishes.

Enhanced Pastoral Plans and Vision Statements

Most parish pastoral plans that embrace change are plain, uninspiring narratives. They can be fortified through the use of numbers. For example, a parish vision of "high-quality liturgies that parishioners can't wait until the next Sunday to attend" becomes more powerful and meaningful with the inclusion of a measure: "The goal is to attract more than 60 percent of all parishioners to Sunday liturgy." Add a dash of hope and prayer, and pastoral plans can truly become energized and relevant.

Parishioners as "Consultants"

Parishioners need to be engaged at every step of the change process so they can see how their ideas and input are having an impact. The role and responsibilities of parish members in providing consultation and feedback on key decisions and parish planning need to be spelled out in written form and made accessible to everyone.

Transparency and Accountability

Be creative when it comes to communicating. One way is post on the parish website and at every entrance to the church a quarterly statement of what is being accomplished by your staff, councils, and commissions, as well as what lies ahead. One parish celebrated its first anniversary of change by creating a wall of tissue boxes—eighteen feet long and four feet high. Each box was wrapped in gold paper and bore the name of a key accomplishment. Sometimes annual parish reports just aren't enough.

The Continuum of Change

Change readiness is the process of forming the key mission-delivery relationships through-out the parish. Change management is the pro-cess of implementing key points of change through those mission-delivery relationships. And those partnerships, in turn, drive the "4 Ps" of purpose, people, process, and performance that are integral to all change and improvement in parish life and ministry.

Change Readiness

During change readiness, the pastor along with lay leaders and staff use dialogue at the individual and group levels to establish a sense of shared identity across the parish. That communication helps to build and reinforce the belief that we can achieve what we set out to do—as long as we're in touch with the hopes and fears, the strengths and weak-nesses of the parish and its ministries. Change readiness is supported by data, research, and analysis and by the other tools and practices previously cited. It also affords the parish a valuable opportunity to grow its social networking infrastructure. This can be done by forming parish neighborhood groups or communities, for example, or through the use of surveys, focus groups, and listening sessions.

It should be noted that many parishes and pastors use pastoral plan development or a capital campaign as the platform for change readiness. This is wrong since they are more appropriately acts of change man-agement. Development of mission-delivery relationships and a shared identity should be considered parts of the change-readiness process (done prior to pastoral planning or a capital campaign).

An effective tool by which a pastor and key lay leaders can assess their preparedness to lead change readiness is described in the graph that follows. It has two dimensions: a fundamental appreciation of the culture of the ordained ("O") and an appreciation of the culture of the laity ("L"). Within this framework, optimal conditions for partnering and for the development of mission delivery relationships exist at the center. High appreciations that skew toward the corners indicate conditions that are not conducive to partnerships and where leadership is hampered in its quest for change-readiness development and change-implementation management.

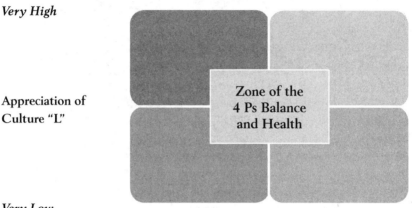

Very High

Appreciation of
Culture "L"

Zone of the
4 Ps Balance
and Health

Very Low

Appreciation of Culture "O"

Very Low   *Very High*

This framework has been used by pastors, finance councils, pastoral councils, and parish staffs to not only map out the current reality and relationships but to track the journey of those relationships and challenges over time and across personnel changes in the parish, including pastors.

The example below describes an actual parish where the pastor operated in the lower left corner, the parish administrator in the lower right corner, and the faith formation director in the upper left corner. The result was an unhealthy, unproductive, and conflict-ridden environment where no change or improvements could occur.

To resolve these issues, the framework suggested that one to three people needed to leave or significantly change how they worked. Neither of those situations occurred. It wasn't until a new pastor was assigned to the parish who operated clearly in the center that two staff members left within six months. Consequently, parishioner registration, Mass attendance, and stewardship rose substantially within a year. And a new pastoral plan was developed, embraced, and implemented within two years.

Awareness to Action System Tool: Catholic Diocese, Parish and School Setting

Role of the Integrators of Pastor, Parish Directors, School Principal, Pastoral Council and Finance Council

The Free Agency Zone

High Appreciation of Laity Culture
Low Appreciation of Ordained Culture

Pastors, principals and directors do not effectively and efficiently manage their core processes, ministries, programs and services with growth of activities with little alignment to Catholic teaching

Individualism, confusion, with groups and people vying for power and privileges in the local parish and school

Experience of staff and parishioners of being left directionless, with little focus on mission, ministry, quality and performance

Catholic teaching with little substance or challenge

High levels of frustration with little focus on mission or ministry and little sense of communion

Growing financial instability and decreasing registered households, stewardship and / or enrollment

Low Appreciation of both Ordained and Laity Culture

The Leaderless and Lifeless Zone

The Political Zone

High Appreciation of both Ordained and Laity Culture

Open conflict and disagreement between councils, pastor, staff, and /or parishioners with local dissonance and noise a predictable and influencing factor

Self-interests overrun roles, responsibilities and relationships

Unity, performance and quality takes back seat to the "show"

Pastors and/or directors maximize "telling" and "controlling" and minimize excellence in staff and parishioner consultation

Departments and Catholic school operate in hard silos with little communication, collaboration or innovation

Resources are hoarded for local benefit, and truthfulness is lessened

Low Appreciation of Laity Culture
High Appreciation of Ordained Culture

Resentment and Passive Aggression Zone

Balance Zone

Pastors and parish leaders recognize the legitimate need for balance between the ordained and the lay authorities, roles, responsibilities, cultures, and gifts.

Differences are not treated as threats, and the local focus is the building of a vibrant Catholic parish and sacramental life, as well as Catholic education at the parish and /or local area

The key focus for shared ministry through distinct roles and responsibilities is the Mission of, and in communio with, the Catholic Church

Source: Team Works International

Change Management

As described above, change management is the process and act of implementing key points of change through mission-delivery relationships, and the shared parishioner identity and parish efficacy that develop. These relationships drive the "4 Ps" of purpose, people, process, and performance that are essential to all change and improvement within the parish and its ministries.

In the graphic to the right, change readiness is reflected in the first two circles of "Individual Identity" and "Parish Identity and Efficacy," while change management is embraced by the next two circles of "Parish Pastoral Plan and Change" and "Individual Transformation."

Parish Pastoral Plan and Change describes the key initiatives of change for the next three years along with anticipated improvements in performance. Detailed implementation plans for those initiatives should cover the first year only and set forth who the key players are, their roles and responsibilities, time frames, and the potential challenges and roadblocks to change. Ownership of action plans should be assigned by the pastor to staff members, councils, and committees, rather than the pastor taking on that burden himself.

Parishes and schools should integrate the key initiatives of a parish pastoral plan into a five-year (or longer) financial model that covers revenues, expenses (including staffing), investments, and fund balances. This long-range financial model should be reviewed and updated semi-annually or quarterly.

Some parish leaders believe that they should budget and spend every incoming dollar of stewardship and gifts. A more effective strategy, however, is to budget no more than 98 percent of last year's realized stewardship or no more than 95 percent of next year's anticipated stewardship.

Parish pastoral plans should be flexible and fluid and updated on an annual basis. They should also look out over a three-year horizon. It's advisable every fifth year to expand pastoral planning by staging a more inclusive event that features parish-wide meetings and communications aimed at involving everyone in the change process.

Individual Transformation

This final stage of change management involves stepping back from the large group focus of Parish Pastoral Plan development and Parish Identity and Efficacy to the individual level where change readiness began. Pastors need to recognize that pastoral plan implementation may be perceived by some staff members, parish leaders, and parishioners as a threat to their sense of being valued, being useful, or belonging to the parish, not unlike the grief that accompanies a personal loss. Indeed, transition and transformation are fundamentally personal (to test this assumption, try changing Mass times on the weekend).

Addressing these sensitivities requires creating opportunities for engagement and expression of ideas and feelings among individuals as part of a shared journey toward a deeper faith and more vibrant parish life. Focus groups, task forces, town halls, and neighborhood meetings, as well as parish-wide surveys, are examples of forums that can stimulate the dialogue, leading to implementation of a viable parish pastoral plan. Keep in mind that a pastoral plan is fundamentally built on shared relationships grounded in the mission of the church, a shared identity as a parish community, and a strong collective determination that "we can achieve what we set out to accomplish." With that foundation, a parish pastoral plan can flow naturally from a robust change-management process to which everyone has contributed and feels an active part.

Contributors

Michael Brough is director of strategic engagement for the Leadership Roundtable. He developed the Leadership Roundtable's Standards for Excellence program and the Partners in Excellence program that provides education materials and training for Catholic dioceses and parishes. Michael is certified by the Center for Creative Leadership to deliver the Roundtable's Catholic Leadership 360 assessment tool. Michael has worked with and trained priests and lay ecclesial ministers across the United States and in twelve different countries. He was a member of the RENEW International Service Team, serving as executive director from 2001 to 2006. He has degrees in social anthropology and pastoral studies and has qualifications in clinical and pastoral counseling and in education. Michael is from Edinburgh, Scotland, and now lives in Chatham, New Jersey, with his wife and their three daughters.

Dennis Cheesebrow is the founder of TeamWorks International in Centerville, Minnesota. He is a leader, organizational coach, and consultant with over twenty years of experience in creating insight, alignment, and action through the power of the FrameWorks™ processes. His experience covers a range of clients across education, government, and faith-based, nonprofit and for-profit organizations. Dennis leverages a broad background and experiences in business, management, marketing, product development, engineering, manufacturing, public speaking, education, and church ministry.

Dennis M. Corcoran was pastoral associate for the church of Christ the King in New Vernon, New Jersey, and for many years, he was a pastoral associate and director of operations at Church of the Presentation in Saddle River, New Jersey. As a consultant, Dennis coaches and provides resources for pastors in a parish setting to ensure success with ministerial and management goals and objectives. He has spoken across the country on many topics, including liturgy, stewardship, and church management. Dennis lives in New Jersey with his wife, Laura, and their four children.

Barbara Anne Cusack is chancellor of the Archdiocese of Milwaukee and has been a judge and promoter of justice for various courts in Milwaukee, Chicago, and the province of Illinois. She has participated in research groups for a number of committees of the Canon Law Society of America and the USCCB. She has lectured and published widely, including "Relationship between the Diocesan Bishop and Catholic Schools," "The Role of Laity in the Church," *Pastoral Care in Parishes without a Pastor*, "Diocesan Structures," and "'In Communion with the Church' as Applied to Catholic Health Care." She has also been a canonical advisor and contributor to the Leadership Roundtable's Standards for Excellence.

Allan Figueroa Deck, SJ, is distinguished scholar of pastoral theology and Latino studies and rector of the Jesuit Community at Loyola Marymount University. He has served as pastor, director of Hispanic ministry for the Diocese of Orange, and founder and first president of the Loyola Institute for Spirituality in Orange, California. In 2008 he was tapped by the United States Conference of Catholic Bishops to establish and serve as first executive director of the Secretariat of Cultural Diversity in the church.

Peter Denio is coordinator for the Standards for Excellence program and CatholicPastor.org for the Leadership Roundtable. He was acting director of the National Pastoral Life Center and served as coordinator of new projects at RENEW International. He has worked as a lay ecclesial minister for almost twenty years and currently serves as a pastoral associate of adult faith formation at Our Lady of Mount Carmel Church in Ridgewood, New Jersey. Peter recently coauthored the chapter "To Youth" in *Vatican II: A Universal Call to Holiness*. He received a master's in pastoral ministry from Boston College and a master's in public administration from Seton Hall University. He and his wife, Mary, live in Fair Lawn, New Jersey, and have three children.

James M. Dubik is a retired army general, former infantryman, paratrooper, and ranger. He holds a PhD in philosophy from Johns Hopkins University and has published over 150 essays and monographs. He is coauthor of *Envisioning Future Warfare* and author of *Just War Reconsidered: Strategy, Ethics, and Theory* (University Press of Kentucky, 2016). He is board chairman and trustee of the Leadership Roundtable and is a member of the Council on Foreign Relations, inductee of the US Army Ranger Hall of Fame, and distinguished member of the US Army 75th Ranger Regiment. He was the 2012–13 General Omar N. Bradley Chair in Strategic Leadership cosponsored by Dickinson College, the United States Army War College, and Penn State Law school.

John Eriksen is managing partner and cofounder of the Drexel Fund, a venture philanthropy fund that invests and partners in the growth of high-quality, financially sustainable networks of faith-based and other private schools to create transformational outcomes for all students and families. Prior to the Drexel Fund, John worked at the Leadership Roundtable with a focus on Catholic schools. In Paterson, New Jersey, he became one of the youngest Catholic school superintendents in the country. John earned a BA in economics, history, and government from the University of Notre Dame, as well as an MAT from the University of Portland and an MPP from Harvard's John F. Kennedy School of Government.

Mark F. Fischer is professor of theology at St. John's Seminary in the Archdiocese of Los Angeles. He joined the seminary faculty in 1990, after six years with the Office of the Diocesan Pastoral Council in the Diocese of Oakland. He hosts a website at www.PastoralCouncils .com. Active in national theological and professional organizations having to do with pastoral planning, Mark is the author of *The Foundations of Karl Rahner* (Crossroad, 2005) and *Making Parish Councils Pastoral* (Paulist Press, 2010).

Carol Fowler was director of the Department of Personnel Services for the Archdiocese of Chicago (1991–2012), coordinating the work of fourteen archdiocesan agencies that oversaw all human resources functions for the fifteen thousand laity, religious, and clergy of the archdiocese. Carol was president of the National Association of Church

Personnel Administrators and has been a member of the board of the Leadership Roundtable. She was also a member of the advisory board of the Center for the Study of Church Management at Villanova University. Holding a DMin from St. Mary's Seminary and University in Baltimore as well as an MA in counseling psychology from the Adler School of Professional Psychology, she is a senior professional in human resources, certified by the Institute of the Society for Human Resource Management.

Paul A. Holmes is distinguished university professor of servant leadership at Seton Hall, teaching moral and sacramental theology since 1988. The university's first vice president for mission and ministry, he later served as interim dean of the university's School of Diplomacy and International Relations and went on to become Seton Hall's executive vice president. He recently completed another five years as spiritual director of Clergy Consultation and Treatment Service, a therapeutic outpatient program for priests that he helped inaugurate in 1992 at St. Vincent's Hospital in Harrison, New York. In collaboration with the Leadership Roundtable, he developed the Toolbox for Pastoral Management in 2009 and has edited both volumes of *A Pastor's Toolbox: Management Skills for Parish Leadership*. Ordained in 1981, he is a priest of the Archdiocese of Newark.

Andrew F. Kelly is director of Clergy Consultation and Treatment Service at St. Vincent's Hospital in Harrison, New York. For more than twenty years, he has been both the clinical and administrative director of this multidisciplinary outpatient treatment program for priests, both diocesan and religious, in both individual and group modalities. He is also clinical assistant professor of psychiatry at New York Medical College. Dr. Kelly lives in New York City. He is an accomplished diagnostician, therapist, and aftercare specialist, assisting clergy in developing healthy responses to the difficult and rewarding challenges of priestly ministry.

Jim Lundholm-Eades is director of services and planning at the Leadership Roundtable, having worked in multiple fields for over thirty-six years, both in his native Australia and in the United States. With degrees in counseling, pastoral counseling, educational administration, and business administration, he has published work (and videos) on church management, strategic planning, and effective presbyteral councils. Jim has also taught graduate-level courses in strategic planning, administration, stewardship, and Catholic school finance at the Murray Institute of the University of St. Thomas in Minneapolis.

Mark Mogilka is director of stewardship and pastoral services for the Diocese of Green Bay, Wisconsin; he is also a member of the Bishop's Administrative Council. With an MA in religious studies and an MS in social work, Mark has served as chair of the Greater Wisconsin Pastoral Planners and as chair of the Conference for Pastoral Planning and Council Development. In 2006–7 he received the Yves Congar Award by the Conference for Pastoral Planning and Council Development. Mark is coauthor of *Pastoring Multiple Parishes* and he has continuously provided ministry on a full-time basis on the staff of diocesan offices since 1975 in La Crosse, Columbus, and Green Bay. Mark is married and the father of four grown children. He also has five grandchildren.

Helen Osman and her husband, John, live in Austin, Texas, after an eight-year hiatus in Washington, DC, where she coordinated communications for the US Conference of Catholic Bishops and shepherded the US visits of Pope Benedict XVI in 2008 and Pope Francis in 2015. She has served on several international Catholic professional organizations' boards and been recognized with their highest honors for personal achievement. She provides communications support for international, national, and local entities, including Ecumenical Patriarch Bartholomew when he hosted the historic pan-Orthodox Council held in Crete in June 2016.

Dominic Perri has created and delivered leadership training programs across the United States. He addresses topics including managing people of different generations in the workplace, using social media to improve performance, and increasing collaboration and teamwork. Dominic has provided strategic planning, leadership development, training, and facilitation to over one hundred organizations in more than twenty-five dioceses throughout the US. He also serves as a consultant to the US Conference of Catholic Bishops' Committee on Communications, assisting with planning, research, and facilitation. Dominic lives with his wife, Patricia, and their two daughters in Forest Park, Illinois.

Paul Spellman is pastor of St. Mark Church in Venice, California. Originally from Memphis, Tennessee, Fr. Paul received an MBA from the University of Southern California and worked for some years as an accountant. At the age of forty, he entered St. John's Seminary and, after six years of study, was ordained a priest for the Archdiocese of Los Angeles in 2001. He was associate pastor of Our Lady of the Assumption parish in Claremont, California, and was then pastor of Holy Name of Jesus Parish in south-central Los Angeles before beginning his pastorate in Venice.

Charles E. Zech is a professor of economics in the Villanova University School of Business, where he has taught since 1974. He also serves as the director of the Center for Church Management and Business Ethics at Villanova. Chuck is the author or coauthor of ten books on church management, including *The Parish Management Handbook*; *Listening to the People of God: Closing, Rebuilding, and Revitalizing Parishes*; *Best Practices in Parish Stewardship*; *Best Practices in Catholic Church Ministry Performance Management*; and most recently, *Best Practices of Catholic Pastoral and Finance Councils*. Chuck is a regular presenter at the annual conference of the International Catholic Stewardship Council (ICSC) and at diocesan events around the country. In 2008 he was a recipient of ICSC's Christian Stewardship Award. He has served as a consultant to a number of US Catholic parishes and dioceses and in 2010 received the *Lumen Gentium* Award by the Conference for Pastoral Planning and Council Development. Chuck is the father of four grown children and lives in a Philadelphia suburb with his wife, Ann.